Jake & Galy

THE FACE OF GOD

Other Books by the Author:
1. Geeta Enlightened
2. Great Women of India
3. Ascent
4. Realised Saints
5. Sufi Odes to the Divine Mother
6. New Millennium Fulfills Ancient Prophecies

THE FACE OF GOD

YOGI MAHAJAN

MOTILAL BANARSIDASS PUBLISHERS
PRIVATE LIMITED • DELHI

Revised Edition: Delhi, 1999

© AUTHOR
All Rights Reserved

ISBN: 81-208-1590-4

MOTILAL BANARSIDASS
41 U.A. Bungalow Road, Jawahar Nagar, Delhi 110 007
8 Mahalaxmi Chamber, Warden Road, Mumbai 400 026
120 Royapettah High Road, Mylapore, Chennai 600 004
Sanas Plaza, 1302, Baji Rao Road, Pune 411 002
16 St. Mark's Road, Bangalore 560 001
8 Camac Street, Calcutta 700 017
Ashok Rajpath, Patna 800 004
Chowk, Varanasi 221 001

PRICE: **Rs. 250**

PRINTED IN INDIA
BY JAINENDRA PRAKASH JAIN AT SHRI JAINENDRA PRESS,
A-45 NARAINA INDUSTRIAL AREA, PHASE I, NEW DELHI 110 028
AND PUBLISHED BY NARENDRA PRAKASH JAIN FOR
MOTILAL BANARSIDASS PUBLISHERS PRIVATE LIMITED,
BUNGALOW ROAD, DELHI 110 007

CONTENT

1.	An Ancient Prophecy Comes True	1
2.	The Shalivahanas	5
3.	Childhood	9
4.	Freedom Struggle	13
5.	Marriage	17
6.	A Young Enterprise	27
7.	Opening the Thousand Petalled Lotus	29
8.	Sahaja Yoga	35
9.	Spreading on the Wings of Love	47
10.	Meeting with "Gagan Giri Maharaj"	61
11.	A Born Architect	63
12.	A Legal Battle	79
13.	Agriculture	89
14.	Divine Economist	93
15.	A Great Patron of Music	99
16.	"With the Sun and the Moon Under Her Feet"	105
17.	Epilogue	111
18.	Appendix	117

WRITER'S NOTE

"If there is a God, what does He look like?" To see the face of God is the seekers' burning desire. But God does not reveal Himself. In the annals of human record, it happened once, in the era of the Mahabharata, when Shri Krishna revealed His Divine form to Prince Arjuna on the battlefield. Moses is said to have heard the commandments of God, but he could not see His face amidst blinding light. Mohammed the Prophet also did not see the face of God, although he had Divine revelations. But God loves His children so much so, that in His compassion He manifests among human beings in their hour of need, as did Shri Rama, Shri Krishna and the son of God - Jesus Christ.

This Book about the Face of God is not the story of creation, nor is it a description of God Almighty; It is an experience of love, devotion and sheer joy with the incarnation of the all pervading power of Divine Love, Shri Adi Shakti Shri Mataji Nirmala Devi. No mortal can possibly know Her multidimensional forms. But whatever an ordinary mortal does see is so breathtaking that his two eyes alone are not enough to see all Her marvels.

I humbly pray for Her forgiveness for the errors and omissions in so inadequately expressing even a single aspect.

When Albert Einstein penetrated the veil of divine laws which are beyond science, he was spellbound. He said; "All I know is that I know nothing, my knowledge is only like pebbles on the sea shore." How can a candle reflect the glory of the sun or a mortal venture to describe the beauty of the Creator? But he can be filled with Her Joy and he can spread it to others.

This biography of H. H. Shri Mataji is an attempt to share that joy.

Yogi Mahajan

1

AN ANCIENT PROPHECY COMES TRUE

In the ancient astrological treatise Nadi Granth, the great Sage Bhrigu predicted the advent of a yoga in 1970. He described it as the commencement of a new transformation in human consciousness (manvanter). The vaivastav (period preceding Kali Yuga) and Kali Yuga itself will end. Then man will rule with his supreme power (it means with his spirit). After the death of a Yogi in 1922 (Venkataswami), a great Maha Yogi will take birth. This Maha Yogi will embody all the divine powers of God (Parabrahma); that is, She will have the Shakti of doing or not-doing (Kartrum akartrum shakti). In previous ages seekers of truth had to take to devotion (bhakti), knowledge (grana), Patanjali Yoga and all such different methods and disciplines in order to achieve the joy of moksha. Thus they could achieve fulfilment of their heartfelt duty of life (itikartavya) and thus get their heartfelt meaning.

In those days one had to undergo a very severe type penance in order to awaken the sleeping Kundalini and to make Her ascend through the different subtle centres. "But by the Grace of the unprecedent method introduced by the Maha Yogi, the seekers will be able to achieve the joy of moksha in their own lifetime spontaneously. They will be able to see the rising of the Kundalini (in Bujander's Marathi commentary the phrase is 'hytasadesi, hystsa dola'). There will be no need to give up the body by living samadhi (a method adopted of shutting oneself in a cave and dying there while in meditation). There will neither be need to leave the body nor to think of one's rebirth."

"The realised soul, through this yoga, will not have to worry about food, clothing, or shelter. Diseases and mental sickness will be completely destroyed and such people will not need institutions such as hospitals anymore. They will have a power to develop their subtle bodies and other powers..." Every one of these predictions is fulfilled in the life work of Shri Mataji Nirmala Devi.

Christ too has said, "I will pray to the Father and He shall give you another Comforter, that He may abide with you for ever." again, "I will send you a Counsellor, Comforter and a Redeemer - the Holy Spirit will teach you all things." The life of Shri Mataji Nirmala Devi is a fulfillment of Christ's promise.

2

THE SHALIVAHANAS

The age of the Shalivahanas was unique in the ancient history of Maharashtra for the extraordinary duration of their rule which lasted for four centuries, from 230 B.C. to 230 A.D. They were great patrons of art, literature, architecture, and sculpture. They promoted commerce and attracted traders from as far away as Rome. They lived for honour and they led dharmic lives.

The heroic spirit of their descendants also manifested in their women. For instance at the demise of her husband one widowed Princess, being forewarned of the impending danger to her infant children, took courage and escaped at mid-night by swimming through the Nandgoan Shigwe river along with her children. Parsad Rao Salve was the extraordinary son of this astounding mother. She brought him up in the highest traditions of head and heart and he developed a compassionate and a dynamic personality. He rose to be a successful lawyer and a master of fourteen languages. Well versed in the arts, literature and science, he also translated the Koran into Hindi. He became a prominent freedom fighter and he later became the only Christian member of the Central Legislative Assembly. In 1920, he married the highly educated Lady Cornelia of the Jadav clan, well-known through Jijabai, the mother of Shivaji Maharaj. When Cornelia was born, her father had a vision that she would bear two great children, hence he named her Cornelia - after the mother of two great French revolutionaries.

The Shalivahanas lived in Nagpur in a rambling bungalow, gracefully touched by the comings and goings of three generations, filled with assorted toddlers and cousins who came to study from small towns. There was always room for relatives and friends. It had a large compound, complete with a badminton court and a vegetable garden.

In the year of grace 1923, on March 21st at 12 noon, Shri Mataji was born in Chindwara, in Central India. Looking with awe at the smiling and radiant baby, Her grandmother exclaimed, "She is nishkalanka", i.e. without any blemish. But Nishkalanka is a boy's name, so the girl was named 'Nirmala', meaning immaculate.

On Easter Monday the miraculous child was baptised amidst great rejoicing. But on the way back home the coachman lost control of the horses, something had frightened them and they reared so violently that the whole coach collapsed. Everybody was desperately anxious for the life of the baby. However the baby was found under the wreckage of the coach, along with a couple of plump ladies-in-waiting, unhurt and smiling as ever.

She incarnated at a very crucial moment of history.
The world was still reeling back from the aftermath of the first world war and the grey clouds of the second world war were already looming over the horizon.
Mother India was crying under the British tyranny.
Her birth was to mark a new epoch in the freedom struggle of Mother India.
Her incarnation is the single, most important event in the evolution of mankind,
ever since the creation of Adam and Eve.

Shri Mataji at sixteen

3

CHILDHOOD

Nirmala spent a very happy childhood and was everybody's darling. All the animals and birds were Her friends. Sometimes She would frighten the maids of the house, for even snakes would come into Her hands to be caressed. Other times She could be found alone in a remote corner of the house, with Her face beaming with inward joy, lost in meditation. Most of the time She was bursting with energy. She would inspire Her playmates in drama, songs and dances. When She played the role of Shri Krishna at the age of seven, huge crowds were enraptured by the sweetness and vivacity of Her playing a feeling of spontaneous and total identification with the deities emanated from the grace of Her acting. At an early age She exhibited an exquisite taste for music and arts.

She loved everything that was genuine and natural. She would go to school barefoot in order to feel the earth. Her father would send someone to pick her up telling them to look for a girl carrying her shoes.

Nirmala spent part of her childhood in Gandhiji's Ashram and he was extremely fond of her and called her "Nepali" because of her Nepali features. Even at that age her great soul was evident to Gandhiji and he frequently sought her advice on spiritual matters. That the message of all the great saints of India is not religion or philosophy but of self-realisation. Thus Mahatma Gandhi wanted to unite all the religions through the essence of self-realisation.

"Gandhiji was very strick - the way he used to make every one get up at four in the morning, have your bath, come for puja. But his quality was that what he said, he practised, there was no hypocrisy about it: also he used to get into temper with people who would misbehave and I used to put some cool water on him; Because I was a little girl, he would really understand it and he used to say 'how is it you keep so peaceful about all such things?' I said, 'that's the solution; Reaction is not the way we can really work it out; forgiving itself solves the problem'."

Shri Mataji recalls, "I had such a good childhood with my parents. They taught us how to be sacrificing. My father was in jail for years. My mother went to jail five times and from huge big houses we were living in huts. But we used to enjoy everything. The feeling that whatever our parents are doing is for our country's freedom. Thus we never thought of the little comforts children ask for; we could sleep anywhere, eat anything and that has given me the lesson that if you have complete dedication and purity about what you have to do, you can achieve it. As Gandhiji said you have to have freedom first. I saw the Union Jack coming down and I saw the Tricolour going up. That was the moment.... it was beyond me, even now I remember those days...."

"When I was born, there was darkness all around. I thought, how would I tell the people and how to give them realisation? Then I felt, I must awaken them en masse. I saw the chakras of the people, their permutations and combinations. I felt that if they come into collectivity, then they will get their realisation."

4

FREEDOM STRUGGLE

When the time came for higher education, Nirmala chose to study medicine. She wanted to know how far man's knowledge extended. However, Her heart was in the country's freedom struggle. Her heart would wrench with pain as She would helplessly watch the atrocities of the British tyranny. Her soul would go out to the martyrs and Her torn heart would express its anguish in tender songs:

Glory to Mother India,

Victory to thee

The whole universe resounds with thy name

Even the green pastures of your villages sing thy praise

When my eyes are filled with tears

and my throat is choked with grief,

My heart is crying out for thy victory.

The smoke from the martyr's pyre rises to meet the sky

Even there his spirit hails thy glory.

Victory to Thee

Victory to Thee.

Young Nirmala bore the full brunt of the freedom struggle. From 1928 Her parents were regularly in prison. They had made a rule that no one was to shed tears on their departure for the jail, as this would be demeaning. Their parents taught the children to share joy and grief alike. There were no dual standards between the society and the home. Though open minded, the children were brought up traditionally. There was no question of superficiality or compromise. In the absence of Her parents, young Nirmala shouldered the domestic responsibilities, from the age of ten. She particularly mothered Her youngest kid brother, Baba.

It was difficult to get admission in the Balakram Medical College, Lahore. There were only seven seats and they were reserved for girls from Punjab. But Nirmala was undaunted. She confronted the principal and said that when you say it is one country, how can you discriminate seats only for Punjabis. The principal was impressed by Her earnestness and gave Her a seat. Later he discovered that he had worked along with Her mother in a Mental Hospital.

Her attention was always on the benevolence of others. In 1942 She spearheaded the student struggle for freedom and was often imprisoned. On one occasion the British put Her on ice to torture Her, but it in no way dampened Her indomitable spirit. She was rusticated from Medical College and could not complete Her studies. The veteran freedom fighter Vinobha Bhave tried to dissuade Her from participating in the freedom struggle, but Her father warned Her to pay no heed to the old man's advice. When the police came to curb the striking students She stood boldly, alone guarding the gate, shouting the freedom slogan and facing the barrels of their guns. The principal of the college was witnessing this scene in amazement and realised Her great Shakti.

5

MARRIAGE

On the most auspicious hour of 7th April 1947 young Nirmala married Mr. Chandika Prasad Srivastava, a prominent member of the Indian Administrative Service. Since the coming of this Griha Laxmi, the career of Mr. Srivastava suddenly took off. He became the Secretary to the then Prime Minister, Lal Bahadur Shastri. The Shastri family immediately took to Her warmth and the Prime Minister would seek Her counsel and comfort. The love between Shastriji and Mr. C.P. Srivastava was later to find expression in a biography, which Mr. Srivastava wrote about him. He rendered a great service to the country through assisting Shastriji in many crises.

When Her husband became the Chairman of Shipping Corporation of India, She would spend Her time decorating the ships, giving them the benefit of Her comfort and love. This was the beginning of Her interest in interior decoration.

In the beginning the in-laws were a little apprehensive as She was a Christian, but the warmth of Her heart soon won them over. She started to decorate the ships in Indian motifs and naming them after Indian heroes. She would cook meals for the junior Officers, and with Her warmth the Shipping Corporation gradually became an integrated family working in harmony. The result was a whopping profit!

Though a very modest person She was perfectly at ease with the London high society. At a diplomatic reception a rather high browed lady kept braging of her husband's high rank. Meanwhile Mr Srivastava joined them. The lady enquired, "do you know this dignitary." Shri Mataji directly nodded in affirmation. Then the lady asked, "How do you know such a big wig?" In bashful modesty Shri Mataji whispered, "he is my husband." The lady turned red. It turned out that she was the wife of a subordinate officer in Mr Srivastava's office.

The U.N. is indebted to Mr. Srivastava for his 17 years of yeoman service as the Secretary General of the Maritime Corporation. He was subsequently bestowed the highest awards by 17 nations and he was also knighted by the Queen of England. In those years Her husband was so very busy that She was often lonely. But She never complained saying, "It is not necessary to spend long hours together, but to deeply enjoy the few short moments of togetherness."

This is one of the ways She manifested Her great concern for upholding the ideal family relationships. The importance of the family is indeed a paramount aspect of Her spiritual teachings and Her own life exemplifies this. Her in-laws adore Her, Her relatives will not leave, Her friends always seek Her. When Her husband was the Chairman of the Shipping Corporation of India, the employees would say, "She is precious like a Mother to us. Because of Her we always felt we were all family members." In the words of Mr. Srivastava, "Ever since we have lived together, constantly Nirmala has been a dedicated wife standing like a rock in periods of difficulties and crisis which always occur in everyone's life. Her attributes are numerous, but I would mention only a few of them. First and foremost is Her straight-forwardness and Her innocence. She cannot sometimes understand the tortuous ways of others. Her heart is full of genuine compassion for the poor, the needy, the afflicted.

Her husband was the only son of an aristocratic family owning some hundred acres of land. But when the new land ceiling laws came; the lands were taken away and all the various branches of the family were confronted with great financial crises. The newly wed Nirmala immediately took some twenty young cousins under Her maternal wing and helped them to find jobs. Later She arranged their marriages. Amidst Her hectic programmes, all relations, close or distant, high or low, are accorded a warm welcome and never leave Her house empty handed. Her attention is constantly on their benevolence and no effort is enough. She specially diverted Her whirlwind tour to heal Her ailing brother Bala Saheb (former High Court judge in Nagpur).

She loves the company of children the most.

"She cannot bear the sight of hungry children - tears flow out of Her eyes. She is generous to the extreme and gives away Her belongings to others with sincere pleasure. She is not attached at all to any material possessions. Her personal requirements are minimal and Her personal expenditure almost nil.

"In Her personal habits also She is most remarkable. She can live in any surroundings and She feels no discomfort or hardship. She eats with equal relish whatever is cooked for Her meals, whether it is cooked badly or well."

Their family life has had its more interesting moments too. Once a merchant tried to bribe Mr. Srivastava. In the guise of a Diwali gift, he left a bottle of whisky wrapped in a box. When Mr. Srivastava returned home from the office and opened the box he was very angry with his wife for accepting the gift. While he was on the phone shouting at the miscreant, his wife quietly poured the whisky down the drain and got rid of the bottle. Afterwards there was peace.

On Her seventy second birthday while paying a tribute to Her husband's honesty She recalled an incident in Lucknow where he was the magistrate - "My husband is another person whose birthday is today. He sacrificed everything for honesty. He was wedded to it. One day I had gone to the library and as I was coming out it started raining heavily. There were no rickshaws and as a government servant you are really poor and can't afford many things. Suddenly I saw my husband coming on a jeep and I stopped him. He said "I can't stop now, I am going for an important work and I can't take you in the government jeep." I said, "does not matter, because patriotism is very important. If you do not have any feeling for your country, you cannot do anything good. Any kind of sacrifice is not sufficient to satisfy that desire to do something for your country."

During the Delhi communal riots a muslim couple knocked at the door of Her (Rouse Avenue) bunglow seeking shelter. Looking at their desperate condition, Shri Mataji naturally gave them refuge. When Her husband returned home he refused to be a part of such a dangerous venture. Eventually, a compromise was reached and it was decided to let them stay in the outhouse. These refugees later became the famous film stars Achla Sachdev and Sahir Ludhianvi. Some years later when Shri Mataji was organising a fund raising event for a charity, Achla Sachdev volunteered her services gratuitously and she continues to cherish the debt.

With family friends at Her Brompton Square house, London

Once a high dignitary had come to their house for lunch. Sir Srivastava wanted to give him a present. Shri Mataji wrapped up a cheap terra-cotta freak which She had picked up from khurja rejects and this was presented to him. Sir Srivastava was appalled that such a paltry gift should be given to a high dignitary. A few years later when Shri Mataji visited the dignitary's country, he personally came to receive Her, and to Her surprise She found the terra cotta freak displayed in a special glass case. The dignitary described it as a rare work of art by nature and thanked Her profusely. In all such situations Shri Mataji would remain silent. Her inner serenity and love would melt Her husband's anger. She would then win him over with Her delicious cooking. The next day Sir Srivastava would return home with a present for Her.

Shri Mataji has two lovely daughters, Kalpana and Sadhana. Both are married. Kalpana has two daughters - Aradhana and Anupama while Sadhana has a son - Anand, and a daughter - Sonalika.

Photograph taken on the eve of the Knighthood bestowed on Mr C P Srivastava. (Daughters Kalpana and Sadhana in the rear).

"Till the sahasrara was opened I used to wear pure khadi. My husband was collector and all that and he is a little fond of clothes, he would say, 'atleast take to something better'. I said, 'this is the best'. I was wearing khadi throughout and I felt great satisfaction because this is my country where people make khadi in the villages."

6

A YOUNG ENTERPRISE

In 1961 Shri Mataji launched the "Youth Society For Films", in order to concentrate and harness the energy of the youth for national reconstruction and development. The main aim of the Youth Society For Films was to patronise and propagate purposeful and healthy entertainment with a view to infuse national, social and moral values in youth through entertainment, particularly through the powerful medium of films.

She wrote a fascinating article which was published in the Souvenir - here is an extract; *"Artists have to raise the public eye to their standards of taste, and not stoop down to the cheap demand of the public and thus surrender their freedom. This can be done by contacting educational and social institutions by the enlightened artists. Through articles in magazines and newspapers, the idea of such artists can be propagated. Through dramas, films and radio talks, people can be educated for the understanding of real art. Thus the dignity of art can be maintained. By coming in contact with the public at large through these societies, the social self of an artist will develop into a keener and a sensitive being. It will react to the slightest unrest in the nation, to the slightest imbalance in the society. If he sees a leper on the street, his heart will pour out with such sympathy that through his art, he can create an atmosphere by which social workers, doctors, scientists and the people in charge of the state will be forced to think of some solution of the problem of leprosy. If an artist finds his countryman being unpatriotic or cowardly, he can, through others, create a deep impact on their minds. Such is the motivating force of an artist. They are the loveliest flowers of the creation, sweetest dreams of the Creator and dearest parts of the human society. Perhaps, they do not know how they are loved, worshipped and followed by their spectators."*

Her idea caught the imagination of many young artists in Bombay who diverted their talent from vulgar cinema to artistic films. She Herself wrote a play "Rat pagal ho gai" (The Night has gone crazy).

She was also a member of the Film Censor Board where She played an important role in protecting the innocence of Indian films during that time.

7

OPENING THE THOUSAND PETALLED LOTUS

The sun had set over the British Empire. The era of world wars was over. The liberated nations were tasting the maiden years of their freedom. But a sinister imperialism was silently sweeping through the human mind, waging a war without arms against the Holy Spirit. The demonic theories of Sigmund Freud had caught the imagination and had set the Western world on fire. Sexual liberation was seen as the solution to all mental problems. In the absence of any dharmic traditions, and with freedom as an ally, free sex became the rage of the Acquarian Age. Hippies, yuppies, punks and new age kids broke away from all the established norms and gave way to the psychedelic culture of drugs, free sex, acid music and cults. The corruption and hypocrisy of the Christian churches only precipitated the adventure. The Youth did not want to hear any more sermons or to play games with society. They were seeking but they did not know what they were seeking. Hawkers from Rishikesh rushed to fill the vacuum, hawking from sex to superconsciousness, to third eye visions, serpent power or whatever could make a quick buck in the name of Yoga.

Meanwhile, India presented a different scenario. Priests and God men had taken charge of God. The gap between preaching and practice had created a duplicity in the psyche. To the other extreme, there were ascetics who practiced suffering to please God.

Thus between the problem of conditioning in the East and the ego in the West, Shri Mataji was contemplating how to give en masse realisation to the seekers of modern time.

She recalled the saying of Guru Nanaka, "How to tell the truth when there is darkness all around?" But in the ancient Nala Damayanti Purana Kali explains to Nala the importance of Kali Yuga, i.e. the modern times. "When the worst of all times (ghor Kali Yuga) will torture Mother Earth, the Adi

Shakti will incarnate and grant salvation to the saintly seekers who are now seeking God, secluded in thick jungles, steep valleys and inaccessible mountains. These seekers will be reborn in Kali Yuga as normal worldly people and in the course of their ordinary lives as house holders, She will give them realisation".

Shri Mataji decided to study what all the God men were doing. When She was visiting Her brother in Jabalpur, a Professor of philosophy, called Rajneesh, saw Her and prostrated before Her, praising Her as the Adi Shakti. But Shri Mataji did not wish to reveal Her self as a Divine incarnation yet.

When he learnt that Her husband was the Chairman of Shipping Corporation, Rajneesh tried to win many favours through him for his many business friends. He kept pursuing Her to see his work, even assuring Her that it would meet with Her endorsement. She eventually consented to visit his seminar in Nargol, near Bombay on May 4, 1970. She was so shocked to see him looting people under the guise of spirituality, that She was completely disgusted.

She spent the whole night on the sea shore contemplating and in the early hours of the morning, the disgust of falsehood and the compassion to save Her children, impelled Her to open the Sahasrara on 5th May 1970.

She described the opening of the Sahasrara; *"I saw the Kundalini, which is the primordial force within us, which is the Holy Ghost within us, rising, like a telescope opening out. And then I saw the whole thing open and a big torrential rain of beams started flowing through My head all over. I felt I am lost, I am no more. There is only the grace. I saw it completely happening to Me."*

This was to be the commencement of Sahaja Yoga, the work that She had come to fulfill, which only She, as the Adi Shakti could accomplish.

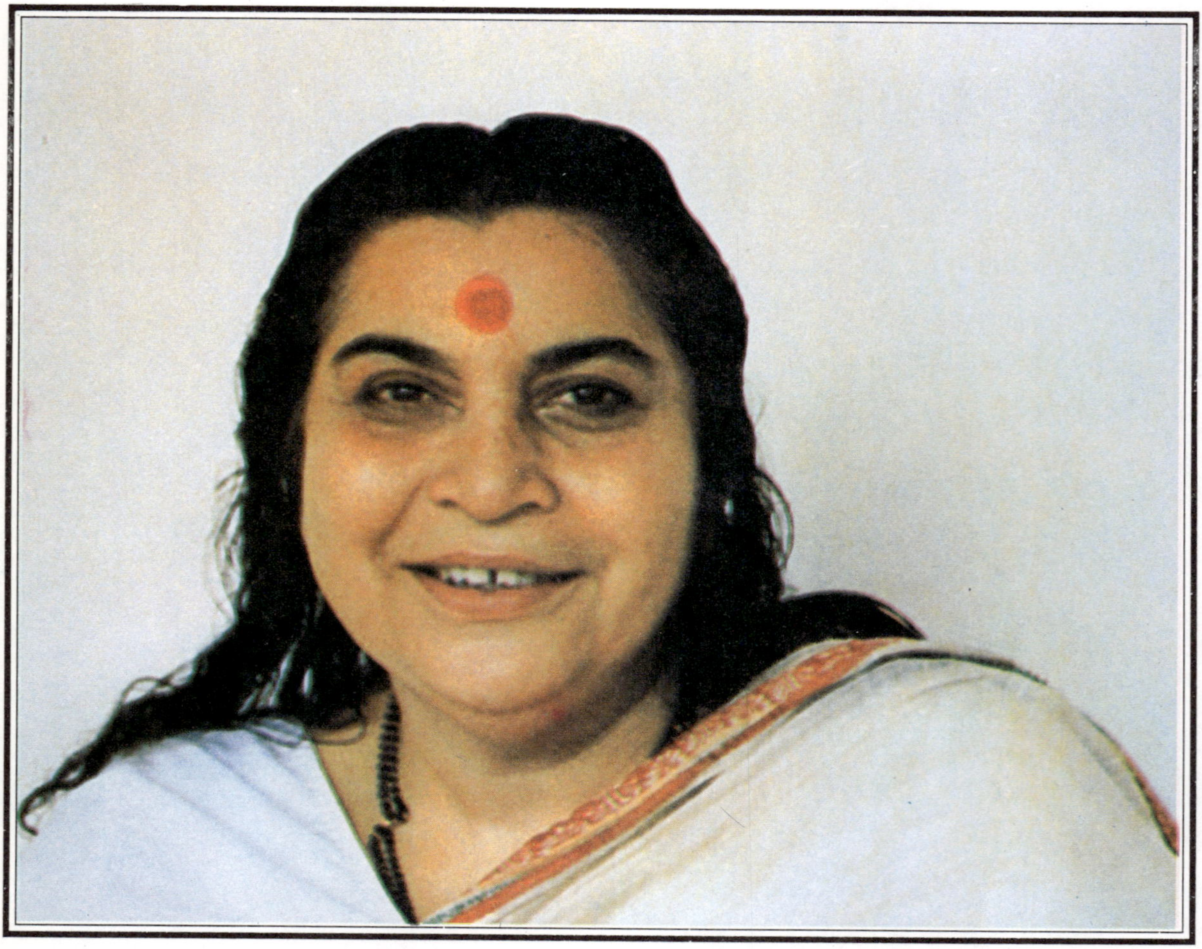

8

SAHAJA YOGA

So far we have only used the power of the ego because we have not known the power of love. Love is the divine power and Sahaja Yoga teaches one how to use it. The mental idea of associating religion with God is a myth. Through religion you cannot connect with God, because religion is only a mental activity. Within us there is no power that can control our abandonment. For instance, there is no power that can stop us from taking drugs, alcohol, etc. But through the instrument within us, i.e. the Kundalini, one can experience the union with the Creator and develop the necessary norms for sustaining it. Sahaja Yoga is the science of connecting ourselves to the mains of collective consciousness. Shri Mataji awakens the Kundalini and connects it to the all pervading power of divine love.

'Sahaja' (Saha + Ja) means born with you (inborn). Whatever

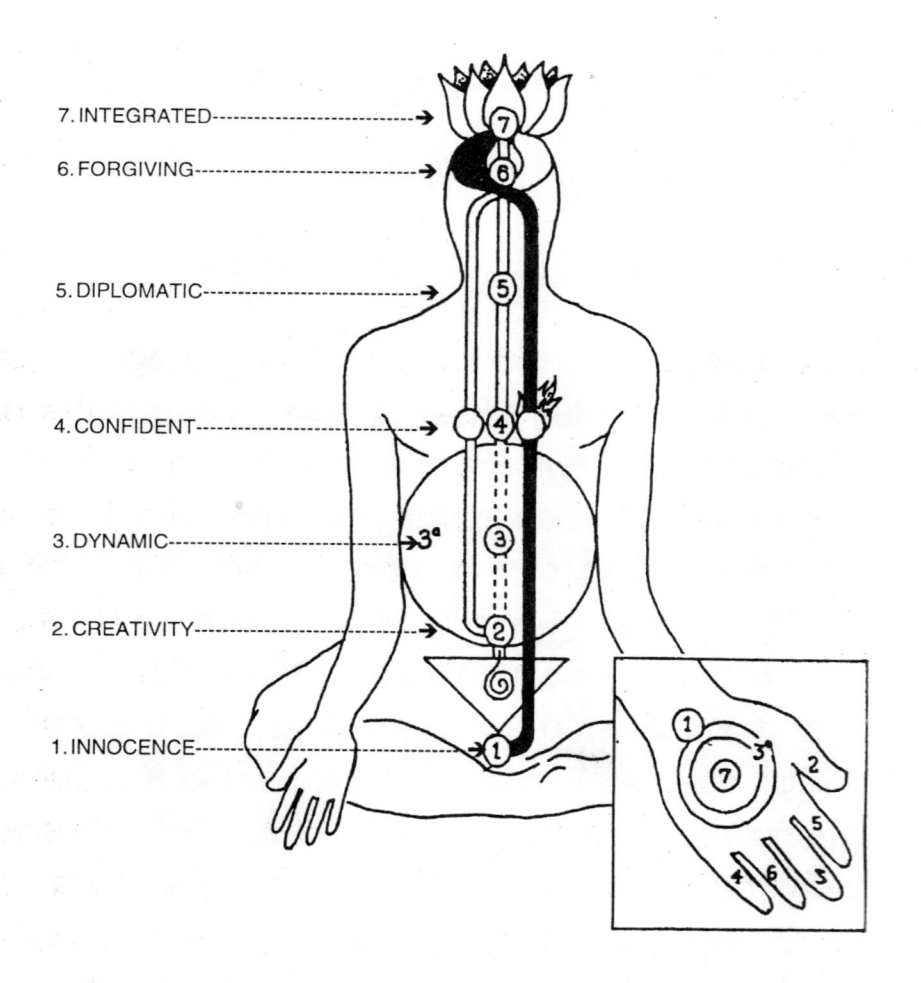

7. INTEGRATED
6. FORGIVING
5. DIPLOMATIC
4. CONFIDENT
3. DYNAMIC
2. CREATIVITY
1. INNOCENCE

**PERSONALITY DEVELOPMENT OF THE CHILD
THROUGH THE SUBTLE SYSTEM**

is inborn manifests without any effort. It is effortless, easy, and spontaneous. For instance, the seed grows by itself into a tree, blooms into flowers and the flowers get transformed into fruit. No amount of human effort can change the process of growth of a seed into a tree. The gardener can only look after the growth of the tree. In the same way, the process of growth of our consciousness to evolve further takes place effortlessly.

When the foetus is in the mother's womb, a column of rays of consciousness emitted through the all-pervading Divine Love, pass through the foetal brain to enlighten it. The shape of the human brain being prism-like, the column of rays falling on it gets reflected into four diverse channels corresponding to the four aspects of the nervous system.

1. Parasympathetic nervous system

2. Sympathetic nervous system (right)

3. Sympathetic nervous system (left)

4. Central nervous system.

The set of rays, which fall on the fontanelle bone (apex of the head known as Taloo), pierce the fontanelle in the centre and pass straight into the Medulla oblongata through a channel (the Sushumna). This energy, after leaving a very thread-like, thin line in the Medulla oblongata, settles down in three and half coils in the triangular sacrum bone placed at the end of the spinal cord (the Mooladhar). This energy is known as the 'Kundalini'.

This subtle energy enters through the centre of the brain (Sahasrara Brahmarandhra) and passes through six more centres on its way down. The gross manifestation of this subtle energy in the Sushumna channel of the spinal cord, is termed as parasympathetic nervous system and the chakras are expressed as plexuses outside the spinal cord. It is also termed as the autonomous nervous system - the system that works on its own - spontaneously. It is a system which is like a petrol pump through which the petrol of Divine Love fills us. But as soon as a human child is born and the umbilical cord is cut, a gap is created in the Sushumna. This gap is known as the Void in the Zen system and the Maya or the Bhav-Sagar in Indian thought.

Later, when the ego and the super ego bloat up like balloons and cover the human brain at the apex of the left and right sympathetic nervous systems, the fontanelle bone gets calcified and the all pervading vital force of divine love gets cut off completely.

Then the human being identifies himself as a separate entity and the consciousness of 'I' (Aham) fatres over. This is the reason why man does not know his 'universal unconscious'. He is served from then on by his ego.

The sympathetic nervous system is created to use this vital energy. There are two systems i.e. left and right. These two channels which carry this energy in subtle form in the Medulla oblongata and are known as Ida and Pingla respectively. The right side system caters to the emergencies of the active consciousness and the left side system caters to the subconscious mind of the psyche. Through the discovery of Sahaja Yoga it has become possible to achieve the transformation of human consciousness to higher planes.

One can see with the naked eye, the pulsing of the Kundalini at the Mooladhar, and also can feel the different chakras existing in the spinal cord with the fingers. Formerly, bridging the gap in the Sushumna was an insurmountable problem but it has been discovered that this gap can be filled with the vibrating power of Divine Love. The Kundalini rises like a majestic mother and breaks the apex of the brain (Brahmarandhra), without giving the slightest trouble to the child (sadhaka).

It happens in a split second, in the short-spell between two successive thoughts. However, if the aspirant is deceased

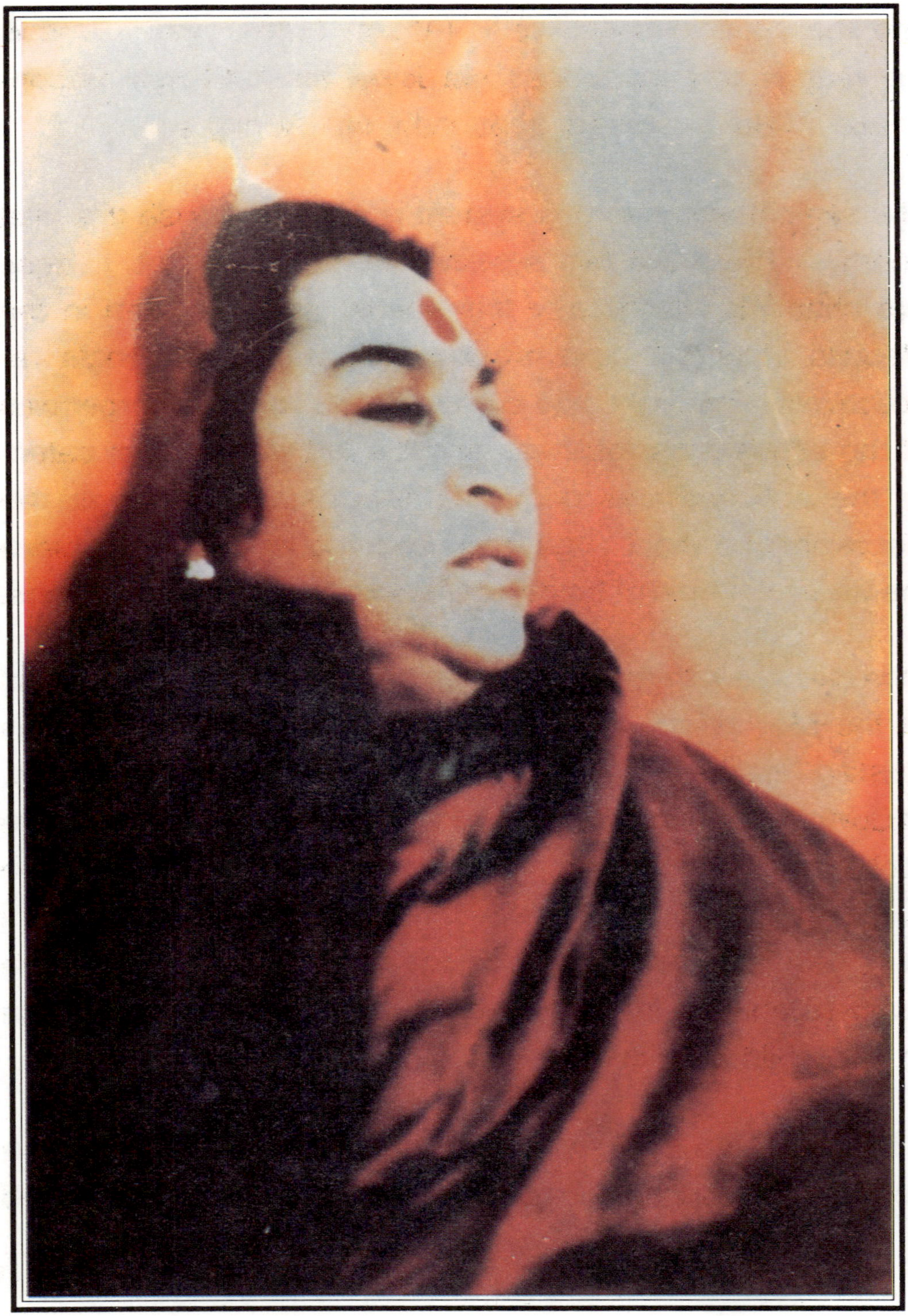

or his chakras are constricted by the over-activity of the sympathetic nervous system, the Kundalini being the Mother of every individual and embodiment of love, knowledge and beauty, knows how to reveal Her love beautifully and to give rebirth to Her children, without causing any harm or pain.

As soon as one's attention moves to one's inner consciousness, one can put one's attention onto everyone else's Kundalinis. One starts feeling the Kundalini, her nature, her position in other people. Collective consciousness is thus established. One becomes a universal being. The power of love is so great and dynamic, that with the movement of the fingers the Kundalini of thousands is moved. These are the signs of the advent of the Golden Age of Truth - the Satya Yuga.

Sahaja Yoga balances, neutralises and heals human problems and relates humanity to the Divine. Thousands of people who have worshipped the Adi Shakti with a pure heart, have been cured of many diseases like cancer, epilepsy, paralysis, asthma, angina, blood pressure and other psychosomatic diseases. Delhi University has granted M.D.s to three doctors for their research work into Sahaja Yoga and it's effects on asthama, hypertension and bronchitis. Prof. U.C.Rai has written a book: "Medical Science

Enlightened" on this research. Presently, research is being undertaken to cure blood cancer with vibrations.

As people started to establish their realisation, they have found that their material problems of income, food and shelter were all miraculously resolved. Even from Her photographs divine vibrations flowed which cured the sick. Yet to the common man She looks like a devoted house wife, content in domestic chores. This is Her Maya, because She is also Mahamaya.

She feels people on vibrations. Often when desciples come to visit Her, even while they are outside the house, She knows who is coming because She starts feeling their vibrations: Also it is possible to pass vibrations to people at great distances either through one's attention or through their photographs. For instance in England She told a desciple on vibrations that his father had a heart problem. When the desciple phoned his mother he learnt that his father had recently suffered a heart attack. Shri Mataji put Her attention on him and the next day he called saying that he had a miraculous recovery.

The absolute truth can be verified through vibrations. If you ask a question and the vibrations are cool; it is an affirmation of truth, whereas if the vibrations are hot then it indicates the negative. For instance, when a question is asked before Her photograph, "was Jesus Christ the son of God" - cool vibrations start flowing or to a question, "Mother are you the Holy Ghost that Christ had said?" - cool breeze, comes on the hands indicating that this is the absolute truth.

In 1995 when She arrived in Thailand the king was very seriously ill. Then Thailand Yogis prayed to her. As she sent her vibrations to him he started recovering. The next day he was well and even walked to wish his mother on her birthday.

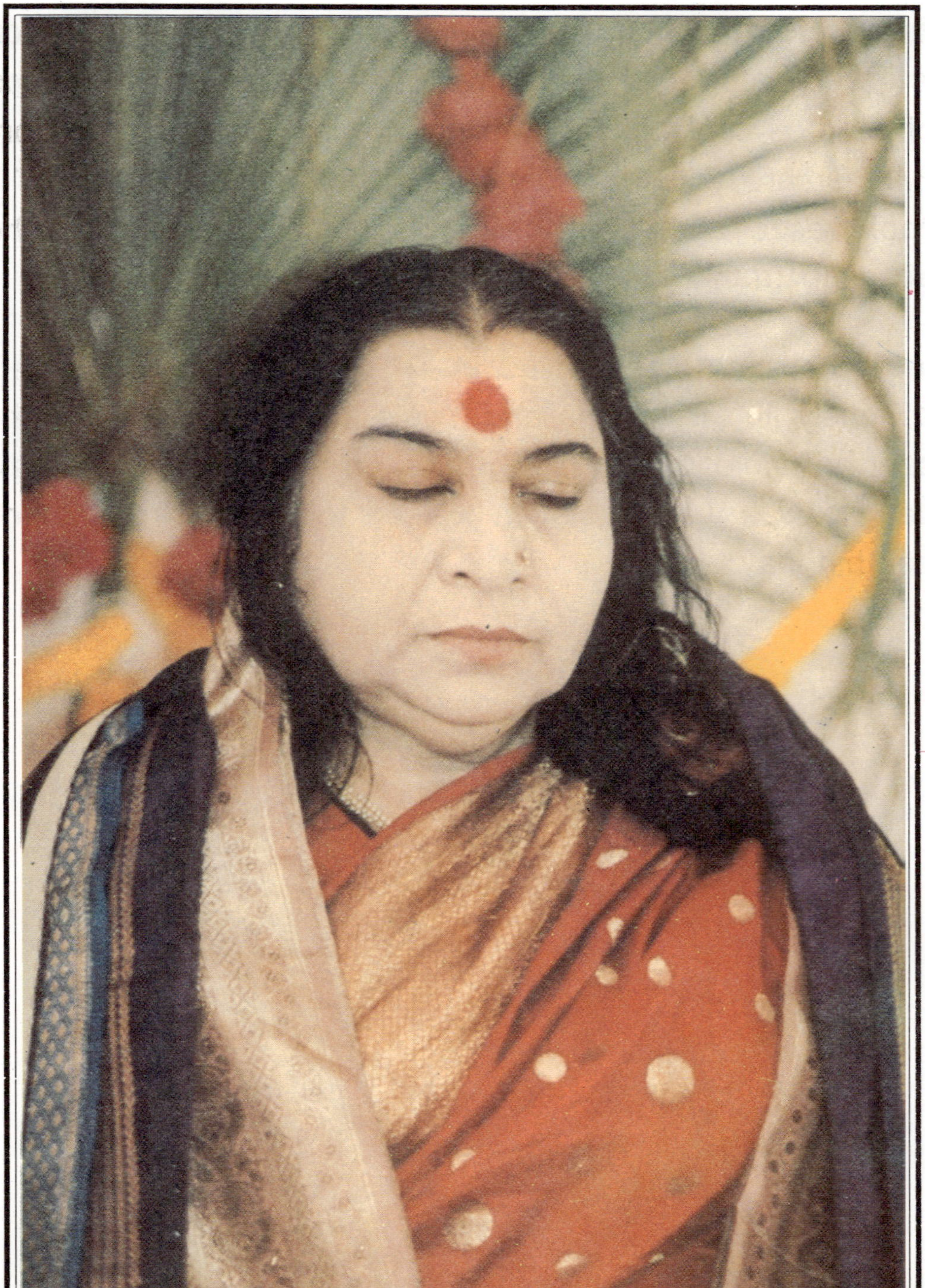

A Letter written by Shri Mataji

The Divine Mother Invites You!

My Dear Children,

What are you searching? Why are you aimlessly and listlessly running about? The joy that you have searched in material gains, the joy that you are looking for in power, the joy that disappeared in the words of books - the so-called knowledge - is all lost in yourself, and you are still searching and seeking! You can pay attention to everything outside, yourself! You are lost in your thoughts, like babes in the wood! But there is great hope that you can rise into the Heaven of "thoughtless" awareness, which we call Self-realisation.

I invite you to this feast of Divine Bliss, which is pouring around you, even in this Kaliyuga, in these God-forsaken modern times. I hope you will come and enjoy the spiritual experience of the Life Eternal.

With all My love and blessing,
Your Mother,
NIRMALA

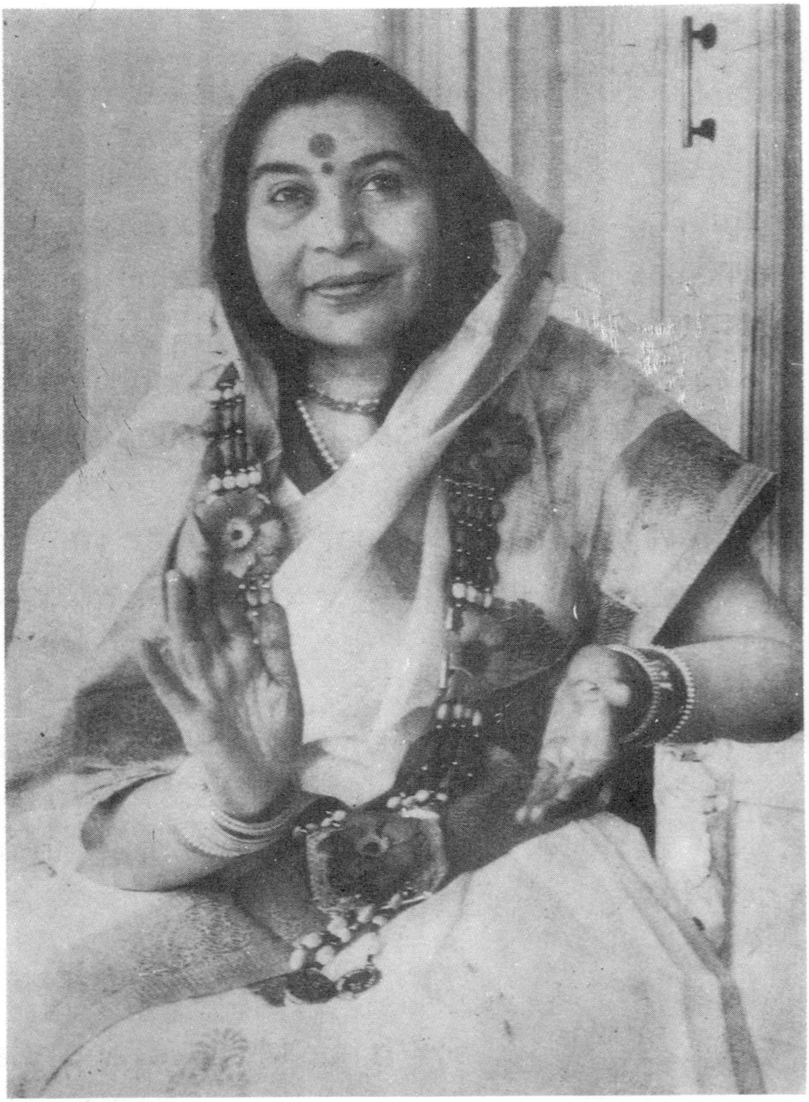

9

SPREADING ON THE WINGS OF LOVE

An old Chinese proverb says, "A ten thousand mile journey starts with the first step". Sahaja Yoga started with a handful of seekers in Bombay and Delhi. Friends would organise small meetings in their homes, where She would give realisation. She would speak very little about Herself but work tirelessly for hours, in establishing the chakras of the seekers.

Gradually She started giving en masse realisation at public programmes. The number of Sahaja Yogis rose to a few hundred and Sahaja Yoga centres were established in Delhi and Bombay. She was not concerned with the quantity of people but with the quality of the seekers. She never took any money for giving self realisation and started Sahaja Yoga with Her own resoure.

She was very anxious to save the American seekers from false gurus, who were leading seekers to their destruction. In 1972 She sold Her gold bangles and with that money, set sail for America. She openly exposed all the false gurus and warned that a deadly disease would result from all the free and perverted sex which flourished in America, but the Americans were too stupified by their new found freedom to pay any heed. A few years later AIDS broke out in America. She was in great anguish at the plight of America and on board the ship to India, Her heart was pining to save Her children,

She wrote;
"To My Flower Children
You are angry with life

Like small children
Whose Mother is lost in darkness.
You sulk expressing despair
At the fruitless end of your journey.
You wear ugliness to discover beauty.
You name everything false in the name of truth.
You drain out emotions to fill the cup of love.
My sweet children, My darling
How can you get peace by waging war
With yourself, with your being, with joy itself?
Enough are your efforts of renunciation.
The artificial mask of consolation.
Now rest in the petals of the lotus flower.
In the lap of your Gracious Mother.

I will adorn your life with beautiful blossoms
And fill your moments with joyful fragrance.
I will anoint your head with Divine Love.
For I cannot bear your torture anymore.
Let Me engulf you in the ocean of joy

So you lose your being in the Greater One,
Who is smiling in your calyx of self
Secretly hidden to tease you all the while.
Be aware and you will find Him
Vibrating your every fibre with blissful joy,
Covering the whole universe with light.

In 1974 Shri Mataji's husband was unanimously elected as Secretary General to the International Maritime Organisation. Shri Mataji set up a house in London and She had to cope with the tedious diplomatic life of endless receptions and official tours. She could not understand the British ego. Amidst hectic diplomatic life, She started Sahaja Yoga with just seven hippies, and for three years She worked tirelessly to save them and She even gave them money for food.

Gradually Her efforts bore fruit, and as prophesised by William Blake, the first Ashram was established in Lambeth Vale.

The building of the New Jerusalem had started. Sahaja Yoga took the quantum leap despite there being no membership, no organisation, no offices or office bearers. It also spread on the wings of love to Europe and Australia.

Every year She would return for a few months and work in the villages of Maharashtra. Her heart was with the Indian masses and the next fifteen years of Her work were confined mostly to villages.

Sometimes She would travel by a bullock cart to one village and then walk to the next village.

She would sleep on the floor or in an improvised cot, eat spartan meals, wash in the river - the comfort of Her body never mattered to Her. It was the comfort of the spirit that gave Her joy.

The land of Maharashtra was greatly blessed by Saints. The people are poor but their spirit is rich and they instantly respond to vibrations.

Starting from Rahuri to Pune, village after village got en masse realisation. She would often take about five hundred western Yogis on a tour to enjoy the vibrations of the various places. When She would return at dusk the sky would be filled with vibrations, forming a pink glow.

By the eighties Sahaja Yoga had grown to all the metropolises. She cured the President of India, Mr. Sanjiva Reddy of a heart problem and he sanctioned land for the first Ashram in Delhi. A Delhi doctor, suffering from paralysis, got completely cured. In Dehradun, an architect suffering from blood cancer, returned from the jaws of death. In Bombay a civil engineer recovered from a deadly liver ailment. Sahaja Yoga had spread all over India through the experience of the people and by word of mouth. There was hardly any media publicity, as there was no money for it. In any case, the Indian press would never have had a good word for something so pure.

In Kuala Lumpur five hundred people came to Shri Mataji in order to be cured of various diseases. She simply asked for the help of the Mother Earth. She made everybody stand barefoot on the ground, and whilest vibrating the Earth, She prayed to Mother Earth to absorb their problems; the earth sucked the negativity and people started to feel relief from their problems, they felt the cool breeze in their hands. In Bombay a man brought his son who was a drug addict, Shri Mataji gave him self realisation, the boy spent the night in peaceful sleep and never again craved for hashish. An alcoholic was brought to the programme by his desperate wife, he stopped drinking overnight. One man who suffered from arthritis was walking away half an hour later. The blind began to see and the deaf could hear. The story of Her miracles spread world wide and Sahaja Yoga took root in South America, Australia, New Zealand, Africa, North America, Turkey and the Far East.

In 1989 the Iron Curtain lifted, thanks to the policies of glasnost and perestrioka of President Gorbachev. Under his unique policy, Gorbachev wanted to introduce a spiritual ideology for the masses. The Soviet Embassy in New Delhi was instructed to study the various Indian spiritual movements. The Embassy sent emissaries to Rishikesh and Pune. Rajneesh got wind of this and he tried to impress the Russians. Meanwhile the Kremlin got hold of a copy of an old BBC release of a Rajneesh Ashram showing group sexual encounters and the Rajneesh proposal was dropped like a hot brick! In August 1989, the Soviet Health Ministry invited Shri Mataji to introduce Sahaja Yoga in order to improve their health programme.

```
                        PROTOCOL
            of intent between the Ministry of Health USSR
            and the Life Eternal Trust International to
            cooperate in the field of Research of Sahaja
                    Yoga Method in the USSR

    Moscow                                    August 9, 1989

          Meeting between Mr. V.I.Ilyin, representative of Main Admini-
    stration for science and medical technologies of the USSR Ministry
    of Health and Mrs. Sri Mataji Nirmala Devi, Mr. Yogeshwar Mahajan,
    Mr. Brian Wells, Mr. Bogdon Shilovysh, representatives of the Life
    Eternal Trust International has been held in the USSR Ministry of
    Health on August 4, 1989. Both sides have drawn up mutual opinion on the
    problem.
    1. Sahaja Yoga techniques proposed by the representatives of the
       Life Eternal Trust International are based on ancient traditions
       of oriental (indian) medicine. These methods may be of great
       interest for different specialists in the field of medicine.
          Broad application of Sahaja Yoga methods in the USSR
       requires profound scientific investigations and clinical trials.

    2. The participants believe it's possible to define specific forms
       for cooperation during 1989.


    V.I.Ilyin                              Yogeshwar Mahajan
    Main Administration                    Life Eternal Trust
    for science and medical                International
    technologies
    Ministry of Health
    USSR
```

The Soviet Union signed a historic protocol with Her Life Eternal Trust, in order to incorporate Sahaja Yoga in their medical treatment.

Within the next four years Sahaja Yoga spread like wild fire. In the metropolises of Moscow, St. Petersburg, Tegliati and Kiev itself, where there are over a hundred thousand Yogis. Her programmes were held in gigantic sport stadia, which were jam-packed with thirty thousand people.

After the breakup of the Soviet Union all the new nations faced severe economic crises. Factories came to a grinding halt and there was acute shortage of consumer goods and food. The western nations were as yet undecided about their strategy. Shri Mataji was deeply concerned and blessed them with the Mahalakshmi principle at a Puja in Moscow on 14 November 1993. The Russians were so touched by Her love, that their Holy Mother had not forgotten about them in their time of need and She came even in the bitter winter to answer their prayers. They worshipped Her as the Madonna. They said, "Mother we have been waiting for You all these years. We knew, from an ancient prophecy, that one day a Mother would come to us from a land in the East to save us".

At a medical conference in Moscow there were six hundred doctors. As She started to speak they requested to have Self Realisation first. The Russian Ambassador in New Delhi honoured Her and thanked Her for helping his country at such a crucial moment.

On 12th November 1993, the Petrovskaya Academy of Science and Arts, St. Petersburg, conferred on Her the Honorary Membership of the Academy.

This academy also conferred a similar award on Albert Einstein, but the President of the Academy remarked that Einstein worked with dead matter whereas the work of Shri Mataji is far greater, as Her work brings peace to mankind. On 14 September 1994 the Academy held a Science Conference with Sahaja Yoga. This was a major breakthrough in the field of science. Eminent scientists accepted Sahaja Yoga as the "Meta Science" and declared that science had not advanced to anywhere near the level of Sahaja Yoga. After Russia, Sahaja Yoga spread to Romania, Poland,

Hungary, and Czechoslovakia. In 1993 H.E. Ayatollah Mehdi Rouhani, who is among the four most highly respected leaders of the Shia Muslims, recognised Shri Mataji as a Divine Incarnation and received his Self Realisation. In 1994 France granted official recognition to Sahaja Yoga as a religion. During Her visit to Brasilia in 1994 the Mayor of the town received Her at the air-craft and presented Her the keys to the city. She thanked him for the keys and, putting them against Her Holy heart responded, "Thank you very much, I we'll put them into my Heart". Ecoforum in Bulgaria awarded Her with a Gold Medal in August 1995 and the same year the Romanian University conferred upon Her a doctorate in Cognitive Science. In Sept. 1995 She addressed the World Women Congress in Bejing.

In public meetings She is open and frank, denouncing the dogmatic ways of life which are detrimental to the spiritual progress of seekers. She says, "I am not here to seek votes, but to tell you the truth. When Sahaja Yogis worry for Her safety, She replies with a reassuring smile, "Love is much more powerful than all the hatred of the world. Do not worry, no crucifixion in this life time. This time the drama is going to be different. Have you not seen how evil people shake before Me?"

Her speeches are not rhetorical but express the tenderest

shafts of Her genuine love and compassion. They penetrate the deepest core of the human feeling. Her concern is intense that after a public discourse in Toronto (1996) She invited the audience to stay back to work out any personal problems. She sat up till 3 in the morning talking to each person individually. This at the age of 75!

One of the least expected and yet most delightful of Her traits, is Her prodigious sense of humour. After public programmes the Sahaja Yogis sit on the floor around Her for hours, laughing and enjoying Her subtle jokes and sparkling wit. The most trivial incident creates a tale of wisdom, a poem of beauty; playfully, effortlessly, opening a precious little corner of the heart. Today Sahaja Yoga is being practised in 65 nations.

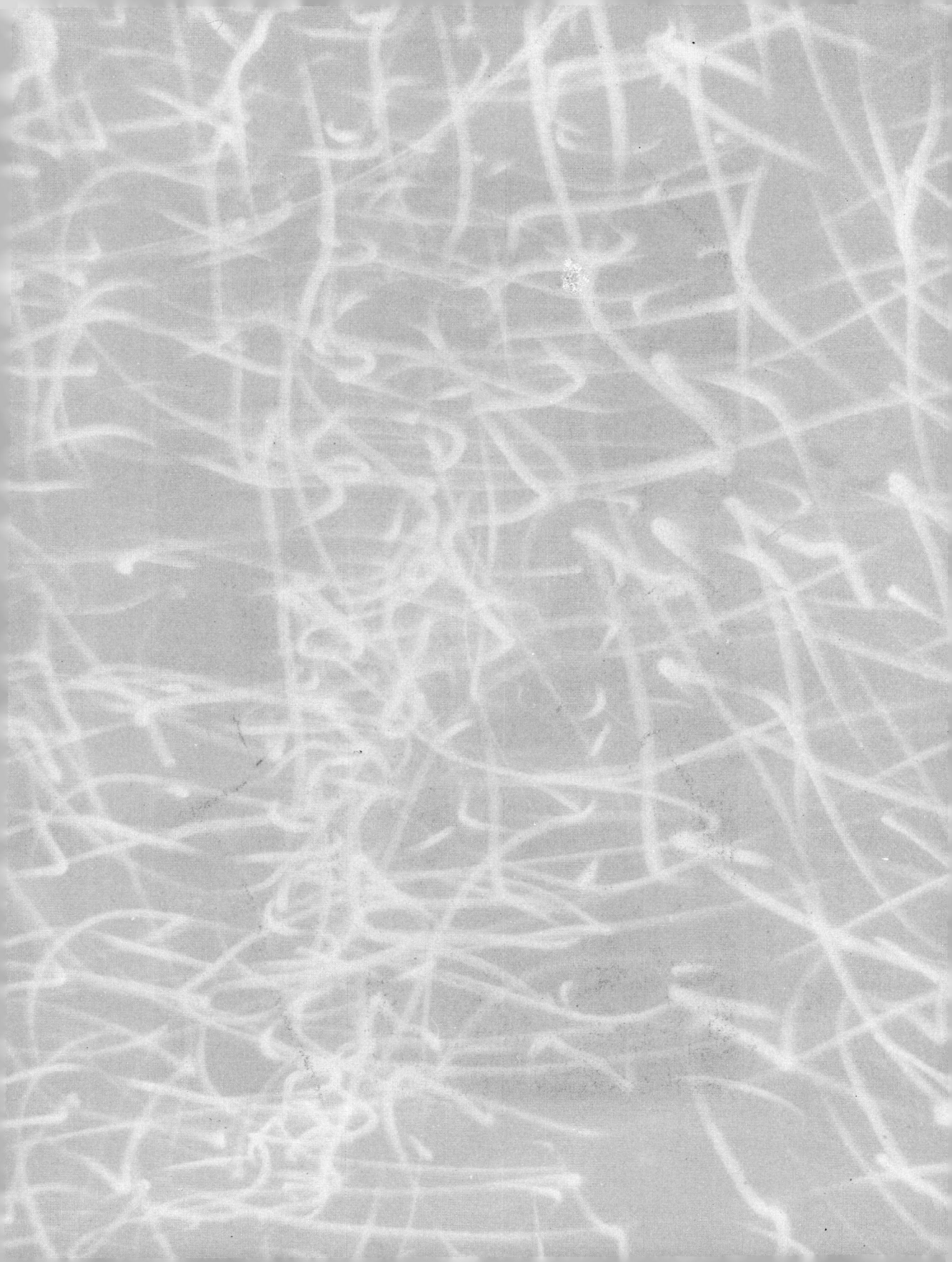

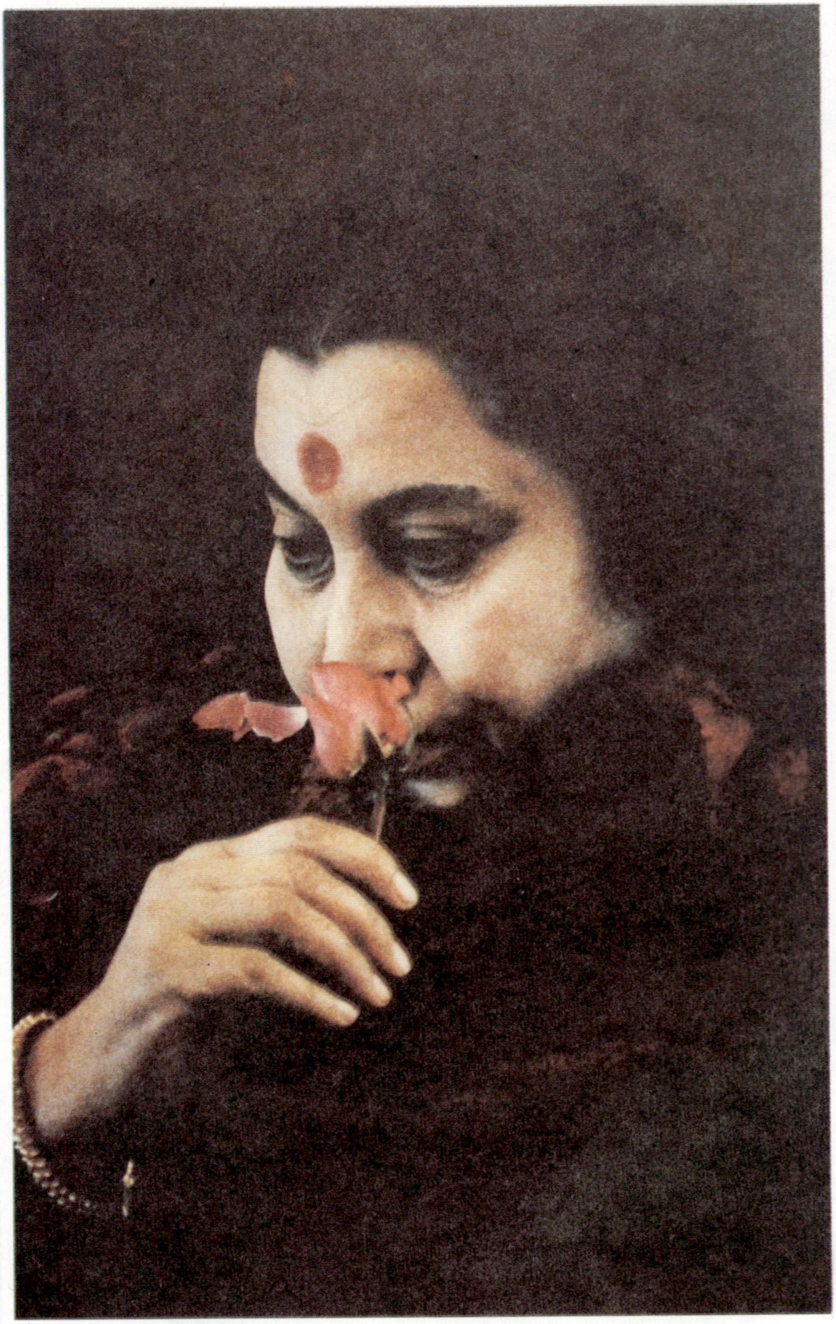

10

MEETING WITH "GAGAN GIRI MAHARAJ"

One day Shri Mataji expressed the wish to visit the abode of a great Sage, Gagangiri Maharaj, high on a hill. This Guru was known for his mastery over the elements.

"Mother why do You want to climb this hill just to see this man?" asked the Sahaja Yogis. "Just check the vibrations" She replied. From the top of the hill came cool vibrations and the Sahaja Yogis recognised at once that this Guru was a man of God. As Shri Mataji started climbing, torrential rain started to pour and She became completely drenched.

One could see the silhouette of the Guru frantically gesticulating, trying to stop the rain. When the Devi reached the place the Saint lamented; "This wretched rain always used to obey me but this time I could not stop it. Mother, why have You taken away my powers?" Shri Mataji smiled,

"You have purchased a saree for Me, now I will have to wear it." The Saint melted away with love. He had also understood that the water dripping from the Devi's saree was vibrated, so was blessing his retreat. She had Her own way of respecting Saints.

Once She stopped at the derelict hut of a very poor woman and thoroughly enjoyed a little meal offered in a dirty pot. Later on some of the Sahaja Yogis asked why She had spent so much time with this beggar? She answered with pain in Her voice "Oh my children do not talk like that about her. She is the widow of one of my dearest sons." Later they learnt from the villagers, that the departed husband was a devotee of the Goddess.

Another time She visited a Saint and sat on the bare ground of his cave. As the attendants protested, She asked with a smile, "Why can't I sit on the floor? I am in the palace of a King."

11

A BORN ARCHITECT

Shri Mataji is a great architect, although She has never studied architecture. She has personally drawn up the plans of two of the finest monuments as well as several Sahaja Yoga ashrams through out the world.

The Ashram in Delhi

Her house in Pune, called Pratisthan, is an architect's dream. Another house in Noida near Delhi, is a marvel. She designed a sprawling ashram with a traditional courtyard in Konkan Bhavan, near Bombay and another in Delhi.

Also a school in Dharamsala, is like a hill fort in the Himachali style (above).

She brings movement into the lines of the building to facilitate the flow of vibrations. Even matter has vibrations, a building should be designed to enhance the vibrations and thus bring peace and joy to its inhabitants. From a building one can feel the vibrations of the architect.

On one occasion a disciple was showing Her a book on Indian Palaces and She asked him to feel the vibrations of each palace. When he felt the vibrations of an old fort of Baroda, the vibrations suddenly became cool. She pointed out that the coolness came because the architect of the fort was a realised soul.

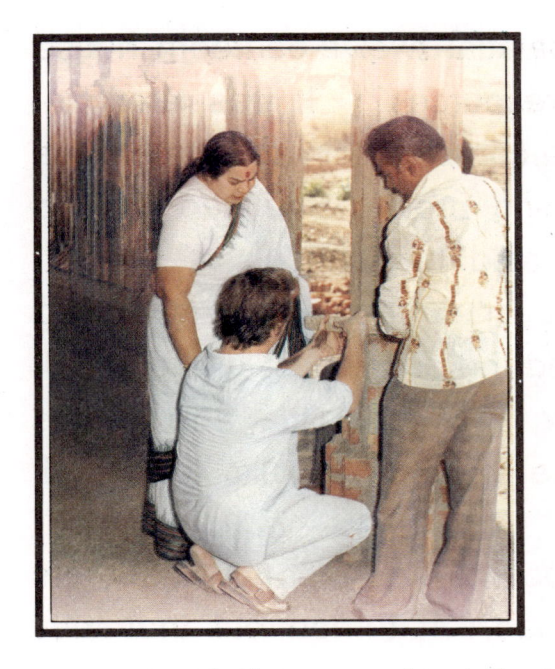

Balance and proportion is the key. A building is conceived as if She is moulding a child into perfect proportion. For Her it is a living process. "A pillar must be bigger at the base than at the top. Entrances must be spacious and regal. A bedroom door should not trespass the privacy of the toilet seat." Her sense of decency and decorum is reflected in each placement. Yet a pragmatic approach compliments the climatic requirements giving way to lavish space, high ceilings, verandahs running around to cool the house and lattice windows to break the strong Indian sun. She resorts to the natural cooling method of cross ventilation by facing all the bedroom windows south, in the direction of the wind.

She has an innate sense of economy which could outwit even the shrewdest economist. She personally visits the source and gets the lowest deals. If wood is needed then She buys it from the forest. One story goes that when She built Her first house in Lucknow, it turned out to be so massive that eyebrows began to rise in bureaucratic circles.

"How can She build such a palatial twelve bedroom house with Her husband's meagre resources?" It was later discovered that She had bought a complete kiln and the excess bricks were sold at a whopping profit. She had leased the river bank for sand and sold the surplus at a profit. After completing the hundred or so doors the remaining wood was sold which covered the entire cost of the wood. Luck follows Her like a shadow. From very little, She creates abundance. Any threshold, over which She walks is blessed.

One day She decided to cook for all the fifty labourers working on the Lucknow house. It turned out that they brought along all their relatives too - so altogether two hundred people were fed, yet a lot of food was left over. Such miracles of Her feeding a multitude from a very limited supply of food often occur. Sahaja Yogis later discovered that by praying to Her as the Goddess Annapurna, their food is blessed and never runs short.

She designed the Lucknow house like a ship, perhaps to familiarise Her husband with the shipping world. It was Her first single handed enterprise. Her husband was the City Magistrate and therefore was too busy. She was quite happy commuting by rickshaws or tongas.

The early fifties were a period when the country was facing

shortages, as India was still in the making after the partition. The house construction ran into problems due to the acute shortage of cement. Her husband would not allow his influence to be used to procure cement, but She was content to face the woes of the common man. The Lucknow house at Nirala Nagar was subsequently given as a gift to Her daughters, who later sold it.

Although She likes traditional Rajput architecture, She blends a variety of styles into it. She is, Herself, very creative and original. She has seen so much of the world and exuberance flows spontaneously from Her style.

For instance the facade of Pratisthan is of traditional Rajasthan stone arches and lattice work, but the back could be Spanish - Portuguese.

Whereas the other two sides the house have equally elegant facades and one cannot tell which is the back of the building.

She spent two years patiently teaching the craftsmen to make Her original ideas tnagible.

With over a hundred skilled and unskilled craftsmen, one never heard Her raise Her voice or get angry.

A correction was made so lovingly that it never sounded like one. Everyone was anxious to please Her. It was like She was cooking a feast and everyone was enjoying it. She would allow laymen and Sahaja Yogis to join in and learn a skill, always encouraging them to attain perfection. Her relationship with the workmen was never that of an employer, but was that of a Mother, mitigating their woes, healing their sickness, bringing clothes for their children. She paid a lot of respect to craftsmen, praising their work and encouraging them with gifts. The workmen loved Her dearly and on weekends they would compose songs to Her. By Her own example She showed how benevolence could form the corner stone of employer-employee relationship. An entrepreneur could be a father figure providing an umbrella of protection to his workers. A Bombay Industrialist Rajesh Shah heeded Her advice and was able to save his steel factory from a ruthless Trade Union.

She would innovate and then spontaneously evolve a new technique. She invented a new device that gave a surface a stone looking finish. It could be applied on wood or plaster and give them a stone appearance.

She explains that art can be very relaxing. A serene work of art does not provoke thought.

In thoughtlessness one becomes silent. In silence there is inward growth and spontaneous meditation. She finds Chinese art inspired by Confucious and Lao Tse, a very deepening experience.

She loves natural material, marble is best for vibrations. She visited the Makrana marble mines to personally select the marble, even though it involved an eighteen hour car ride along the rough Rajasthan tracks. She supervised the laying of the marble floors and matched every vein in the marble slabs and created a work of art. At such moments one could see how the Goddess made nature so beautiful. She likes variety and uses a range of different materials, stones, slates, colours, styles and accessories not only from India but from all over the world. There were five architects working under Her at Pratisthan but they could not match Her infatiguable energy.

Since the land at Pratisthan was at different levels, the architects planned to reduce the plinth to zero level. She instantly foresaw the waste of resources in doing so and overnight changed the plans, taking advantage of levels to make the house more interesting. She taught the architects how to take advantage of a disadvantage. This was to be Her hallmark in every crisis. The architects eventually surrendered to Her and recognised Her as the ultimate architect, confessing that their real training started under Her. It is now ten years since these architects became famous and prosperous, owing their success to Her blessings.

Alhough She is always open to new ideas, She will never compromise Her values. During Her absence the architects had built the main staircase like a narrow tunnel, quite unbecoming of the house. On Her return She ordered its demolition, much to the dismay of the architects. She then rebuilt a grand staircase in pink marble which today is the pride of Pratisthan.

Her mind is so fertile and creative that it is far ahead of the times and is impossible to keep pace with. It travels faster than the speed of light. Her attention penetrates like a laser beam. Even for a split second if Her attention catches something, it absorbs it completely.

Once while travelling from Pune to Srirampur, Her eye caught a fleeting glance of some white rugged stones on a hillock. On Her return to Pune, She sent for Wagonloads of the stone for cladding the exterior of Pratisthan.

All decorative arts in Her building ascend to a crescendo of exuberance. She explains that the spirit expresses Her joy in exuberance. The western mind is too busy so it is exhausted and cannot bear exuberance, thus it takes to blank wall in tones of white and grey.

Perhaps She is the most widely travelled person in the world. She has seen so much. This, combined with Her tremendous power of creativity and genius gives birth to a unique style of architecture. For Her, architecture is like clothing the universe with myriads of colours, forms and continums. It is like Her face which is a mirror reflecting Her intense feelings of love, compassion, joy, radiance, majesty, grace, tenderness, tears, concern, motherliness, bashful modesty, triumph, laughter and usually playfulness. Also when necessary She can put up a show of terrible anger for the benevolence of Her devotees. Her moods can vary like Nature; from tranquil snow peaked Himalayas to the gushing ganges who must purify the world of its woes and give solace in the work of the mighty occean. She is the eternal witness, witnessing Her own play, art, architecture, decoration are the enjoyment of that play. A colour added to accentuate something, a shade toned down to hide something, a curve added to give movement or a line drawn to bring balance and proportion. Her creativity brings out the choicest virtue and then She bejewels it. When virtue shines then it also spreads and overcomes all the thorns of negativity. Indeed, as God made man in His own image, that image has to be embellished. This is Her job and She has succeeded even beyond all expectations.

Pratisthan is an artist's paradise, decorated with intricate carvings, statues, frescoes, cornices, lattice work, murals, stain glass fountains and gardens. Every door is carved and every room bears Her personal touch. It is a blend of a variety of styles which do not conform to the western notion of monoism. The mood could swiftly change from Royal Rajput to ethnic or from Victorian to oriental. There are no dark corners. It is Her leela, full of surprises. Each room commands a spectacular view, wherever one turns, the warmth of the Mother thrills the heart. In Her buildings

She gives a new heart to the universe.

Herself, a very informal person. She says, "A house should not be like a hospital". She is not fussy about anything. Her grandchildren and visitors are indulged in Persian carpets to antique furniture in Her salon. If a guest happens to appreciate a ming vase or an old ivory carving, She insists on presenting it to him. Her followers are well aware of Her immense generosity and are mindful not to express their appreciation too profusely, lest She presents them with the item. Though She enjoys beauty, She is not attached to material things. To Her the sharing of Her love is most important.

She will spontaneously take off a solitaire and give it away.

Once at a Sahaja Yoga wedding in Ganapatipule, a girl arrived at the last moment for her wedding without any ornaments. Shri Mataji took off Her gold bangles and put them on the bride. When the bride came to return them, She had forgotten all about the matter and refused to accept them. The left hand does not know what the right hand gives. One day She sat down to calculate the amount She had spent on Pratisthan. It turned out that a quarter of it constituted gifts She had bestowed on people - watches for the workmen, tape recorders for the masons, vehicle for the architects, etc.

She loves to cook for the Yogis.

Though She is very generous in giving gifts, with great difficulty She accepts gifts. She has the most exquisite collection of art and curios, but She treasures the smallest gift offered to Her and praises it from Her heart. Everything is carefully kept with love of the desciple who presented it. She never forgets the gifts given to Her. Like showing something to a guest She would add, "so and so gave it to me twenty years ago." She is very caring to Her disciples. One evening while serving Her tea, a disciple spilled the tea on Her beautiful saree. He was of-course very upset. To comfort him She deliberately spilled some more tea on Her saree and said, "see, even I can make a mistake. Don't be upset, I was going to change My saree anyway." On another occasion while travelling to a social function one disciple got left behind. Half way down the road She turned back to pick him up. She personally takes care of the comfort of every disciple, 'did some one receive them', 'have they eaten' 'do they have proper accomodation'. She even makes their menus and gives recipies for their meals.

She never cares for Her own comfort. Moving between small flats in Pune to oversee the construction, She would spend a day at the site, have a packed lunch and take a short rest on a cot amidst hectic activity.

Sometimes She appears oblivious of Her body and She

forgets to eat. It becomes necessary to persuade Her to eat something. She does not worry about what She eats but if a guest is invited then She produces a banquet for a King. She loves to cook for the yogis, and has even compiled a book of Her own recipes. Her son-in-laws fondly narrate anecdotes when their mother-in-law cooked chicken biryani or minced meat. Her husband's favourite are Her sweets. She says that when you love someone then you know what he likes, and you enjoy making it.

That is how She enjoys building houses for Her children without feeling tired. She does not feel that She is doing anything. Within days She will undertake whirlwind tours of Australia or some other far corner of the world and will return bursting with energy. Between these many tours and night dashes to Bombay, She built a twenty thousand square foot palace at Pune at the age of 68.

With a beaming smile She responds, "people say I travel so much, but I am just sitting there, I don't think I travel. I am sitting there as I am sitting here, I can sit anywhere - just not to think.... and remain in thoughtless awareness."

An interesting account is given of the ancient site of Pratisthan in one of the Maratha ballads which runs as follows :

"The city of Pratisthan is the jewelled head ornament of the glory of Maharashtra and is beautified by pleasure giving palaces and chaityas soothing to the eye.
It contains 68 sacred places for the public,
and as within its walls fifty heroes were born,
it was called the city of heroes."

The description aptly applies to the new Pratisthan from whose foundations will arise a new world of the Divine Spirit.

12

A LEGAL BATTLE

In 1986 Shri Mataji decided to move residence back to India and Her husband also wanted to take an early retirement from DMO. She wrote the following letter to Her disciple, Shri R.D. Magdum, who is a Civil Engineer, to acquire farm land;

Smt. Nirmala Devi
48 Bromton Square
London
dt. 5th April 1986

My Dear Mr. Magdum,

This is in reference to your letter saying that there is more than half an acre land absolutely stony and useless for agriculture. It does not matter as I am in the process of buying 7 acres of adjacent land, so we will have altogether 11 acres of land for farming.

I have confirmed the following points again, as given by you;

1. The farm house does not need collector's permission. (The copy of the letter written by the collector to Mr. Malhotra is with me).

2. The farm house has no specific dimensions. Mr. Dhumal sent a registered letter to the collectorate, however no reply has been received for over two months.

3. The permission has been granted by the Gram Panchayat. (Confirmed by Gram Panchayat that only they are authorised to grant the permission).

4. This area is a green belt and has to be used for agriculture only.
   The farm house can be used by us also for the agriculture storage, etc. We have got permission from the planning department.

Now as my husband is going to retire very soon, I wish to plan the house as per requirements for my family and my daughters' families. Both my daughters are married in the 'Shetkari' families. Specially the younger son-in-law, who is the grandson of our late President Rajendra Prasad, belongs to a very well known farmer's family of Bihar and himself is a farmer. Both son-in-laws will be staying with us and take to farming. I am also negotiating for farmhouse very near Paud which is a few miles from our farmhouse. All our agriculture activities are going to be operated from this farmhouse. So to begin with, in our plan please include the following suggestions, made by my son-in-law.

1. Large garages for modern agriculture equipments like tractor, etc. 5 numbers.
2. Godowns, 6 numbers at least measuring 11 x 22'.
3. Cow sheds altogether measuring at least 44 x 22'.
4. Large court yards and verandahs for cleaning and drying.

We have a very large house in Lucknow but is occupied by Govt. (Indian Oil Co.) and they are not willing to release though they are paying a nominal rent and are settled nicely even when the contract is completed long time back. (Thanks to my husband's policy of patronizing the Govt. we cannot buy a flat as my husband has no black money).

So now we have to settle in the farmhouse in Pune. Whatever money we have we will spend in farming lands, in this farm house and in buying modern equipments.

You have seen our London house and you know our life style. Though I am 'Shetkari' and a sadhu baba, I can live in a hut, however My family has to be comfortable. My husband, who has worked for Indian Government for 40 years, should retire in a comfortable place. For your information we have never lived in a very small house. We would not like to live in the city anymore, but would help us to live near our farms in our old age. Please note that though there are no restrictions about the farmhouse, still do not go beyond any stony area as farming is the main object of our stay in the farmhouse. Please plan spacious bedrooms for ten persons; My husband and Myself, two daughters, two son-in-laws and four grand children. Also a common large hall for sitting and dining, one large in-door room for children to play. There should be at least two guest rooms of large sizes. My husband's guests are all high international officials, so we do not wish to cut a sorry figure.

The facade of the house should be Indian Art and interiors should be Rajput style (as you know we are descendants of the 'Shalivahanas' - who ruled in Paithan (Pratishthan) for thousands of years. They were Rajput kings who migrated from Rajasthan.

We give a very poor image of our 'Shetkari' to the outside

people. But whatever farmhouses I have visited so far, have been enormous, for example, my father-in-law in Khairabad, my son-in-law's farmhouses, Mr. Dhumal's farmhouse in Veer, Raja Patil's farmhouse near Ichalkaranji, Usha Patel's farmhouse in Dandeli, Raul Bai's in Dhule Dist. Yogi Mahajan's farmhouse in Pathankot and Dharamsala - all of them are one bigger than the other. You may visit one of them, most of them are 4 to 5 stories. Of course you should never treat that as a model, but better visit them to find out what is the capacity. I cannot give you any particular idea. Still the house should be as big or as small as you think proper.

Our farmhouse should be placed on the edge of the cliff and as it is the stoney area, according to your letter, it may cost more money but it will serve two purposes. Firstly, you will save good agricultural land and secondly, we can watch the agricultural activity in the valley (which land I am definitely purchasing). Furthermore, you may have any number of stories, as there is no definition, I think two stories may be sufficient.

As you say that it is absolutely legal to have a farm house without any restrictions, still I would request you to use only stoney area. If the stoney area is more than your requirement we can increase the court-yards or you may add a storey if stoney area is inadequate.

Also please make the structure facade as I would like to spend more on the interior and the exterior. Pune is full of ugly flats and heavy decor. I would like to bring some delicate jali work from Jaipur to create a new dimension in farmhouse building. So some people at least will spend money to make some beautiful houses. Also it should give a sense of dignity to my other shetkari friends to spend on beautifying Maharashtra instead of wasting money on drinking and dancing in the clubs with other urban wasters. So that they can leave something for the progeny instead of pseudo-modern culture. Also if our farmhouses are made interesting the young people would not run to the city and become clerks instead of becoming dignified shetkari's children.

This kind of farmhouse indeed would be expensive but much less than a horrid Bombay flat. I hope every farmhouse could be decorated differently with handicraft as you find them in the remote villages. This is my dream for the villagers who have nothing to look forward or to hope for. My father who was the member of the Constituent Assembly had a dream that the villages must develop first, there should be a 'wada' for a farmhouse for every shetkari, very well decorated and interesting so the children should not.

run to the city but should become shetkari like their father. I hope this happens one day, though this has happened already in China which I have visited and seen how the Chinese adopted Gandhiji's methods to improve their villages.

I hope you do not mind this very long letter from Me. I am sorry I could not talk to you on the phone at this length, but I had to explain as there is no information written down about a farmhouse. You know I have very different attitude towards My property than many people. We could have had a very modern house which may be very comfortable but I always think that these houses are without any feeling. They do not represent our deep culture of dignity and art. I have already asked Mr. Patankar to study the Rajput art and get Me sketches of their arches and trellis work. I wish you get some books on this subjects. Whatever money I would spend on this house I want to create a feeling of Indian home rather than a mundane boring London house. I hope you understand my way of looking at things, in these aspects specially.

With all my blessing to yourself and to your family,

Yours affectionately
Sd,/-
(Mataji Nirmaladevi)

On the day of Vinayaka Chaturthi, 5th November 1986 the structure was completed and Shri Mataji named it Pratisthan, after the capital of Her ancestors, the Shalivahana Kings (now modern Paithan).

Meanwhile a conspiracy to demolish the farm house was being hatched by a Pune builder along with some politicians because they did not want any farming activity in this area. The ruthless Pune builder and his mafia wanted to convert this beautiful green valley into the strip of Las Vegas on the pretext that the land was unfit for agriculture. In Maharashtra there is a funny law that agricultural land cannot be used for buildings unless an amount is paid to the administration and its permission obtained. This has led to a lot of corruption which has given birth to a mafia with a political nexus.

Shri Mataji's plan for farming to help farmers with more productive seeds and vibrated plants thwarted the mafia plan.

The mafia prevailed upon the administration to cook up a case that Pratisthan was not a farm house but a temple and that the land was unfit for agriculture. A show cause notice for demolition was served on Her on 25th March 1986. Simultaneously, a frontal attack was launched through concocted and slanderous reports published by Sakal newspaper to malign Shri Mataji in every possible way. The Collectorate treated Shri Mataji as a criminal, probing into Her bank accounts, making inquiries if She had used public money to build the temple. When they checked Her bank account they found that all the money had come from Her husband's foreign exchange account. Even the Charity Commissioner was approached to investigate to find out, if any money had been siphoned off from The Life Eternal Trust.

Shri Mataji was undaunted and went to Court which granted a stay on 2nd May 1987. The mafia retaliated by inducing the administration to post a demolition order on the gates of Pratishthan on 7th May. Her attorney again obtained a stay against the demolition on 18th May. But the administration secretly got the stay vacated on 27th May exparte. The next day Shri Mataji arrived from New Zealand and barely had a day in which to save Pratisthan.

Overnight She dictated a petition to the Bombay High Court. On 28th May the Bombay High Court granted a stay, observing that, "Prima facie the impugned order of the additional District Judge is a negation of the well recognized right of a party to be heard before any order to detriment is passed .... Demolition of structure stayed until further order." On 4th November 1988 the Bombay High Court passed a decree in Her favour. Thus single-handed Shri Mataji fought in the Courts and vanquished the adversary thus revealing Her mastery in temporal law and Her skill as an astute lawyer.

During the legal proceedings She displayed a quick grasp of the law. Her sharpness in catching the point and rebutting it, amazed the lawyers. She was prepared to argue the case Herself in Court. What is most surprising is that She had never even seen a legal document before, as Her very efficient husband took care of all such matters. He has in fact a double doctorate in law, but in this case he was far too busy in London and She did not want to trouble him. Her multidimensional personality is like a multi-faceted diamond, where a facet shines when the light of Her attention falls on it and it reveals all the information.

13

AGRICULTURE

"All living work is done by God Almighty. You cannot even sprout a seed. The seed has to be put in the Mother Earth for germination." But Shri Mataji can sprout the seeds and revive dying flowers. In 1991 Her flight arrived in Sydney very late and She could not accept the flowers from hundred of Yogis who were waiting to welcome Her. Next morning She sent for the flowers but they had all wilted. She put them all in Her bath tub and vibrated the water. By evening the flowers were fresh and blooming, as though they had just been plucked. She feels the growth of all living beings on Her own parasympathetic nervous system...... "those the gladioli are losing too much energy, better pinch open the buds, those roses need more sun, that plant is dying, raise its vibrations..." Plants and animals respond better to Her vibrations than human beings, perhaps because they have no ego.

She set up a research farm in Pune. With vibrations, one sun-flower became over one foot in diameter and the agriculture department became interested in Sahaja Yoga methods. The Government of Maharashtra granted Her land at Neera Narsingpur to experiment in Sahaja Yoga methods for producing non-hybrid seeds. Hybrid seeds may give an initial boost to the yield, but the seeds are far too expensive for the poor farmers and also they have little resistance to virus. Huge amount of chemical sprays are required which cost a lot of money. Shri Mataji increases the potency of the non-hybrid seeds dramatically simply by soaking them in vibrated water. An Australian scientist at WHO took up this method and his research showed that fields irrigated with vibrated water bore twice the yield over fields that were irigated with ordinary water.

The yield of indigenous cows was also improved by giving them vibrations. It was found that the vibrational quality of milk from the Indian cow was far higher than in more exotic breeds.

In 1982 the Rahuri Agricultural University gave a special grant for making green trees for Maharashtra. Shri Mataji has also advised Russian agro-scientists on how to improve their agriculture with vibrations.

Shri Mataji loves flowers and has brought plants from all over the world. In 1993 She produced tulips in Pune for the first time and the roses from Her farm won many prizes in flower shows. The process of tissue culture has been revolutionized through vibrations in Bangalore.

Sahaja Yoga methods are bringing a silent revolution in agriculture, through giving self realization to farmers and thereby bringing them joy and prosperity.

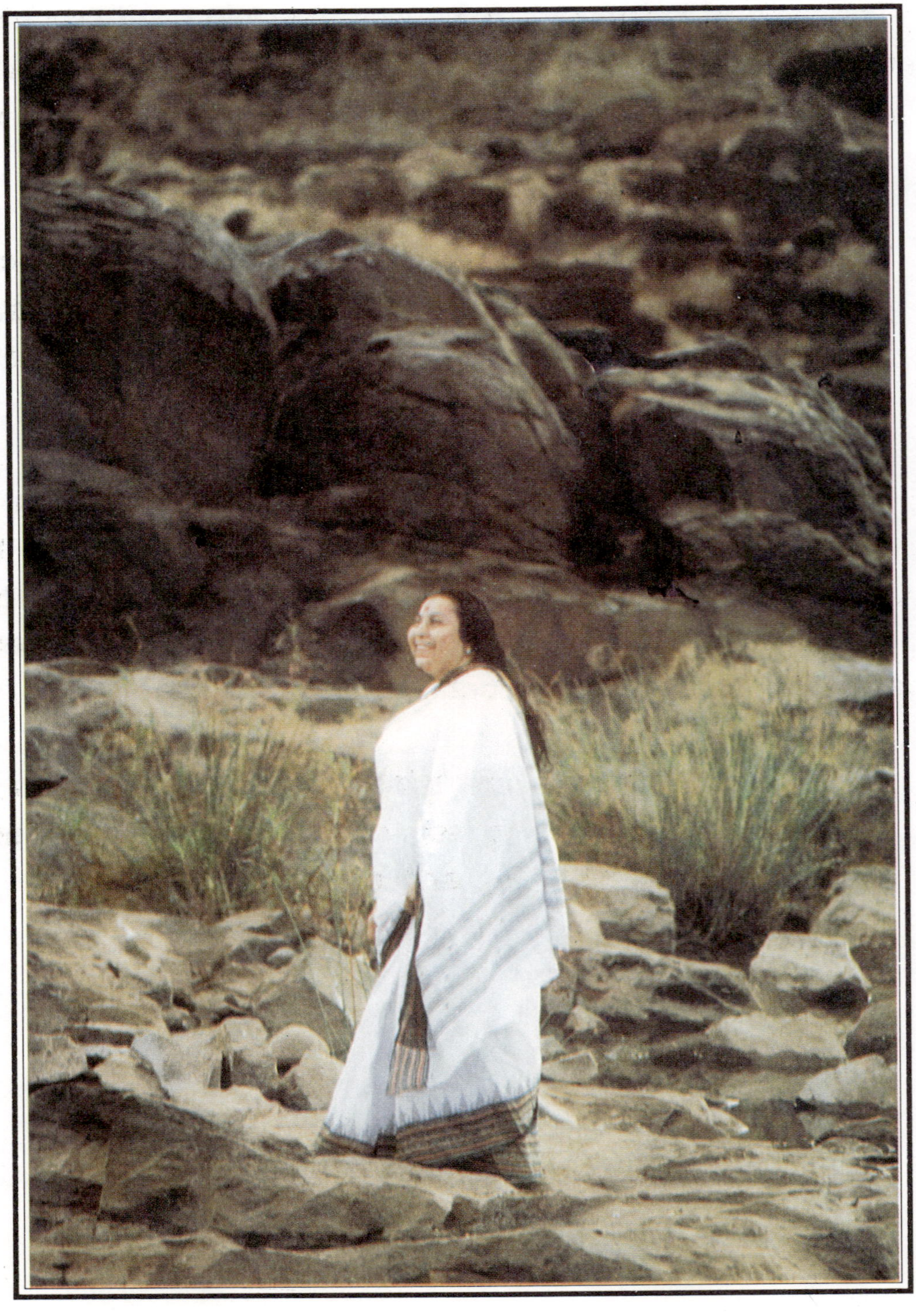

14

DIVINE ECONOMIST

In Her modesty She says that She does not know how to draw a cheque but She once caught a highly reputable London Bank napping when they missed out on a foreign exchange transaction during a steep fall in the exchange rate. Although She does not believe in share speculations, She makes very profitable investments in real estate for Her husband. Often She scans through a balance sheet and points an error to the embarrassment of a Chartered Accountant. These are but a few attributes of the Mahalaxmi. She once gave some valuable advice to the Finance Ministry for liberalisation of the Indian economy. The Finance Minister has great respect for Her wisdom.

In July 1991 Shri Mataji was looking to buy a castle in northern Italy. An Italian art dealer offered his castle near Milan but demanded fifty percent in advance of registration.

Shri Mataji insisted on registration of the sale deed prior or at the time of payment. The art dealer claimed that he was unable to do so as his daughter who was a partner in the property, was on vacation. All the Sahaja Yogis were taken up by his charm and the grandeur of the castle, but Shri Mataji held Her ground firmly and eventually the deal fell through. It was later discovered that the dealer was a crook and Shri Mataji would have lost all Her money. Her foresight and judgement of people is absolute. After that no one dared to argue with Her or to question Her judgement. Shri Mataji finally purchased a more spacious castle in Cabella for a quarter of the price.

The Castle in Cabella, Italy.

She is like a mirror that clearly reflects the state of the human mind. One learns more about oneself through Her eyes than through self analysis. She knows everything about a person yet responds like a naive person. Often there are people from varied walks of life sitting in Her company, with each one She is at perfect ease and communicates at his wave length. With a child She will ask the name of her doll. To a farmer She would enquire after the harvest. With an old friend She would be very intimate. As a dutiful wife to Her husband She would tenderly say, "Its a little chilly, take my shawl". To Her daughters She would enquire about their shopping. With Her grandchildren She would discuss the latest teenage fashions. To the ministers in the Kremlin, She will discuss how to improve agriculture. To a probing press reporter's question, "Who are You Shri Mataji?", She laughs and replies, "Better get your realisation first, then you will know who I am."

All these manifestations of Her personality are spontaneous. She never plans Her talks. The text of each talk pertains to the prevailing situation spontaneously. From these observations one can understand how the All Pervading Power of Divine Love takes care of everything and protects us. How it works only She knows. What does it matter how electricity works? It is better to use it. Her interests are so varied that She is interested in everything and in everyone's welfare.

Unemployment in India has been Her greatest concern. To help the craftsmen She began marketing their handicrafts in Europe. She innovated their designs for the European Market and is now running flourishing enterprises all over Europe selling terra cotta, porcelain, ceramics, brass, wood carvings, costume jewelry and other handicrafts. Thus Her compassion reaches out to the poorest of villagers. She has seen enough money being siphoned off from charities and so does not support the idea of giving alms. It is better to give employment, medical help, quality education, good seeds to the farmer and to improve the output of the Indian cow with vibrations.

She says, "We should not try to copy others and get their products on our head which are just plastics. We should try to help our own country. Every portion of every country if it grows, the whole world will be strengthened. Better keep to natural things because this artificial domination of matter kills our spirit."

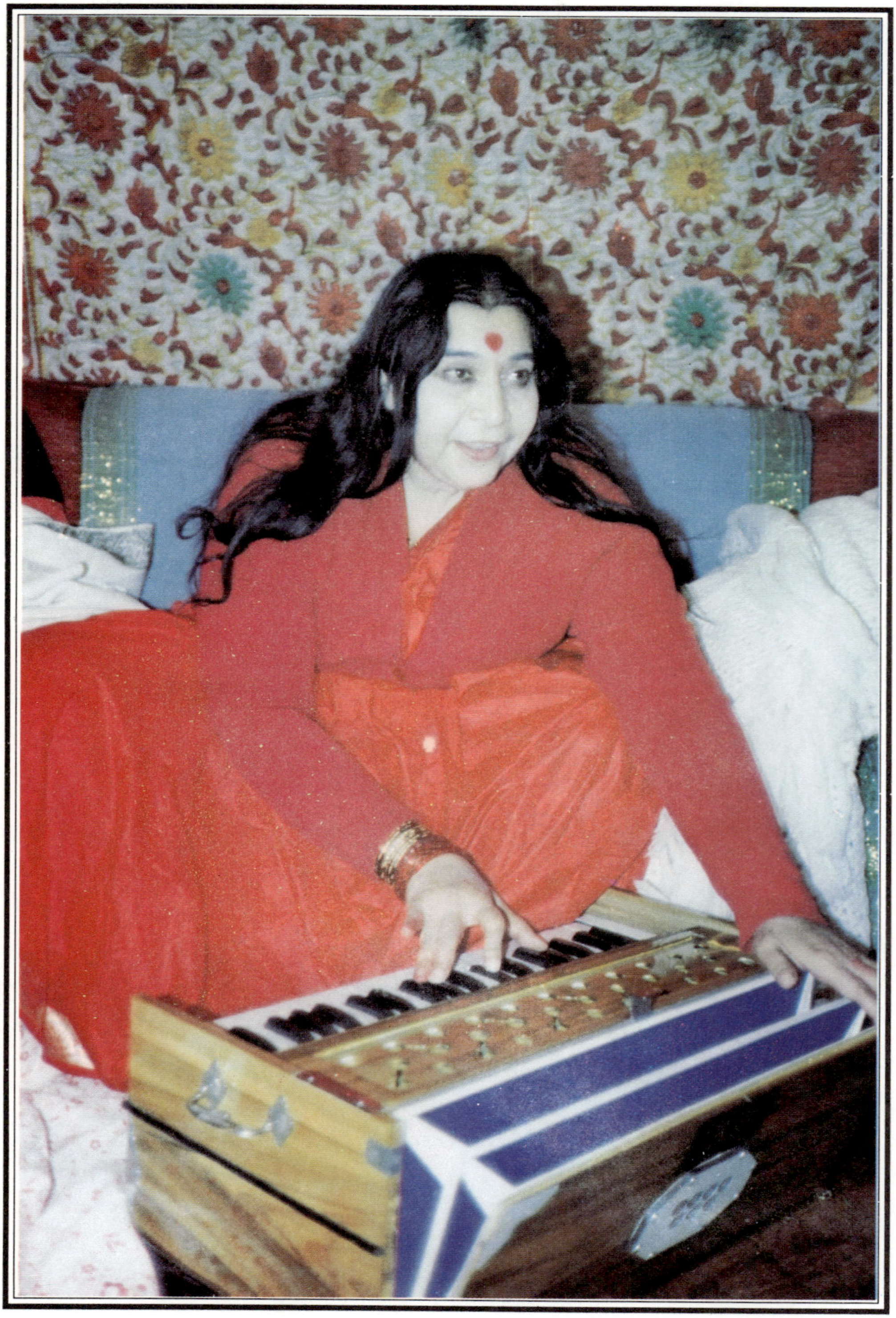

15

A GREAT PATRON OF MUSIC

A great patron of the arts and literature, Shri Mataji played an important role in reviving classical music. She found the vibrations of modern stone music very damaging to the chakras and the brain cells. People addicted to acid music often suffer from loss of memory and disorientation. Whereas the vibrations of classical music, composed by realised souls in praise of God are very soothing to the nervous system (chakras). After self realisation, a musician plays from the Sahasrara and the Kundalini rises. This produces a sympathetic effect on the listener, relaxing and elevating him.

After self realisation the latent talent in the artist blossoms. Many amateurs who received their realisation in the eighties have become great masters To name a few, Prof. Debu Choudhuri, his son Prateek Choudhuri, Ustad Amjad Ali Khan sahib, Hemlata, the famous playback singer of the

Indian film industry. Arun Apte, Ajit Gadkade, Murdeshhwar, Sanjay Talwar, Deepak Verma, Simple, the music group 'Nirmal Sangeet Sarita', the Noida group, Baba Zaheer and his qawals from Hyderabad, Ustad Shafad Hussain Khan Sahib. There is an interesting anecdote about Ustad Shafad Hussain sahib. In 1985 as an amateur he performed before Shri Mataji. A few years later at a concert in Pune a great tabla maestro took the house by storm. Shri Mataji was feeling his vibrations and remembered that She had given him realisation but he had transformed so much that the other Sahaja Yogis did not recognize him. After the performance he came to Shri Mataji and touched Her feet, thanking Her for the blessings.

She has great respect for artists. After a seminar in Pune, She was a bit tired. A vocal recital was arranged for the evening, but everyone prevailed upon Her to take a little rest also as he was an obscure artist. When She retired She heard his voice from Her bedroom. She immediately rose saying, "I have never heard such a voice" and surprised everyone by a sudden appearance. Later with Her blessings this young musician grew up to be one of the most celebrated musicians of India, Arun Apte.

On another occasion in 1996 at a cultural evening in Moscow the programme carried on to the early hours of the morning.

In an attempt to curtail it the organisers cancelled some items. When the programme concluded Her glance fell on some dancers in the audience and She enquired why they had not performed. When She learnt that they had been left out due to time limitations, She instantly announced that She would not leave till every artist was given a chance. Thus the programme prolonged for another two hours!

All the Indian masters look forward to the opportunity to perform for Her. They describe it as a Divine experience where She transports them to another plane where even they do not know what they are playing ... the musician becomes the music, the artist becomes the art. Many great musicians like Bhimsen Joshi, Pandit Jasraj, Praveen Sultana cherish the memory of a such rapport. In fact the vibrational level of music in Her presence can never be reproduced. Perhaps through the sensitivity of an artist, it is easier to recognise Her Divinity. Once when Praveen Sultana was performing for Her in Bombay someone requested her to sing a cheap film song. She rebuked, "Don't you know before whom I am singing."

Once Ustad Bismillah Khan Sahib was travelling by train from Switzerland to Paris when he met some Sahaja Yogis. When he learnt that they were going to see Shri Mataji, he got so excited that on reaching Paris he requested to perform for Her. He recalled what an honour it was to render before Her, but he also complimented the Yogis as being 'walis' or saints. He was amazed at how westerners could have such a rapport with him. It was an interaction of devotion to the Goddess for both.

A talent is a gift from God for spreading His message. The artists realise this and only perform in dedication to Her, but She insists that they accept the boon of Mahalaxmi from Her that would bring them fame and prosperity. "Even for those who come empty handed, She charts the course of their destiny."

Unlike other yogas, Sahaja Yoga is full of joy which is expressed through music and dance. Sahaja Yoga Pujas are celebration of the triumph of the Goddess. Each year Yogis from all over the world gather on the shores of Ganpatipule for seven nights of dedication, devotional music and dance. The Poet Rabindranath Tagore had foreseen this event when he wrote, *"On the shores of Bharat will gather men of all races to anoint the Holy Mother."*

En masse marriages are performed between couples of all castes, creeds and nations, in traditional style. Sahaja Yoga does not create a dry person, but a personality full of vitality and joy of the spirit.

Sahaja Yogis enjoying Wedding preparation with vibrated Haldi.

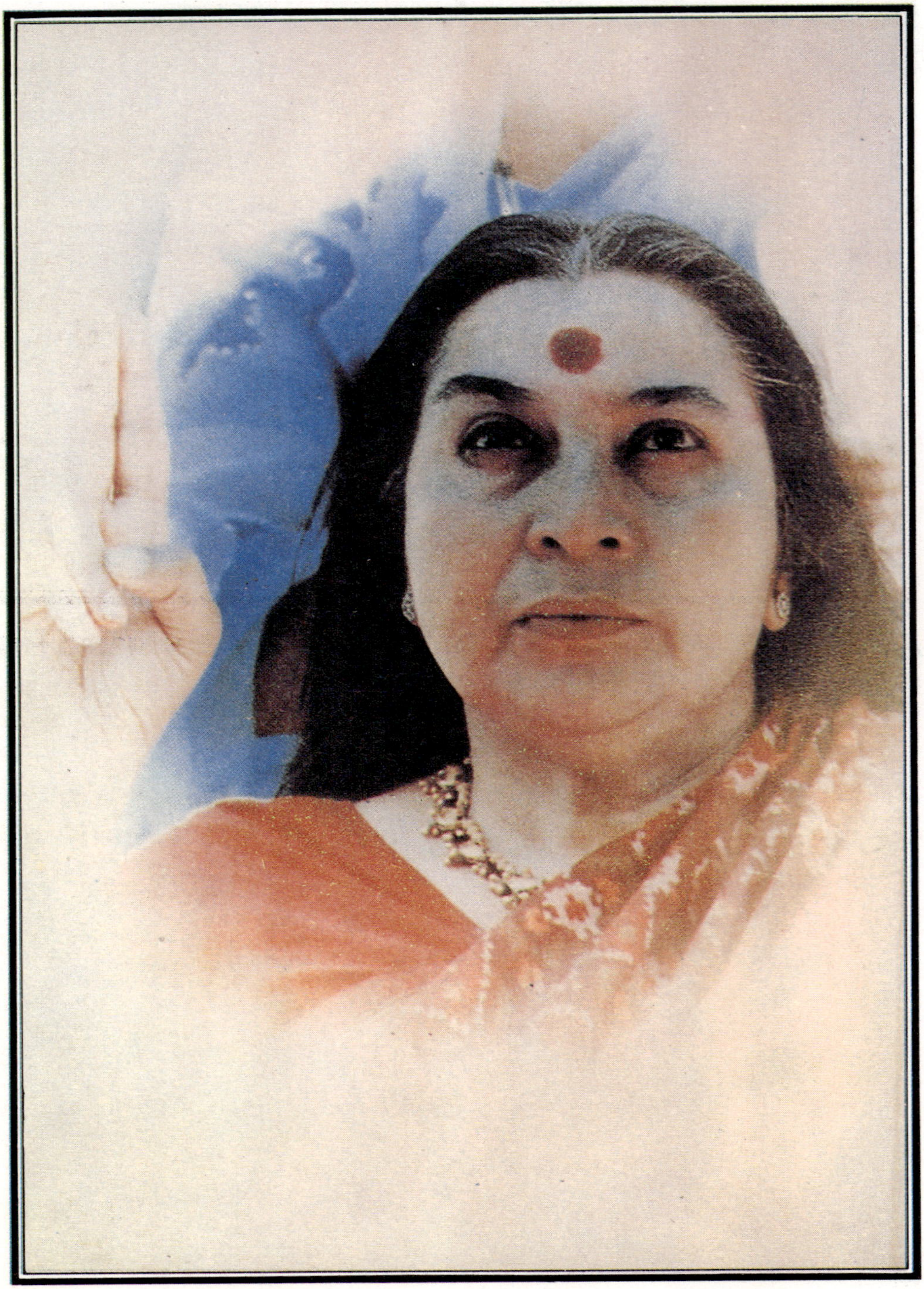

16

"WITH THE SUN AND THE MOON UNDER HER FEET"

"And there appeared a great wonder in Heaven: a woman clothed with the Sun and the Moon under Her feet, and upon Her head a crown of twelve stars" .. *Revelation 12:1*

She has such a photogenic memory that She can recall any incident from Her life with accuracy. Although She never actually studied Sanskrit or Hindi She can, off-the-cuff, recite verses in Sanskrit. She has not read any scriptures but She can quote from them. When She was correcting the Geeta Enlightened for Yogi Mahajan, She knew the meaning of all the sanskrit verses and even made correction in sanskrit where the author had erred. The light of Her wisdom transformed the title from "Geeta" to "Geeta Enlightened". Where does Her innate knowledge come from? With a little sense of perception one knows that it can only be Divine Knowledge.

On many visits to ancient temples and monuments She would recall the whole history of the place during one of Her previous incarnations. When Her brother accompanied Her to the ancient ruins of Feha, Persepolis in Isfahan, Iran, She recalled where the doorways to the throne of Indra were, where the courtiers sat, etc. She remembered every detail of it as though She had lived there just yesterday. Even the guide was amazed and learnt many new things from Her.

Once a group of western Yogis visited the place of Shri Sita's bath called 'Sita Nahani' near Nasik. When the local people showed the spot of the bath, She remembered from Her previous incarnation another site of Her bath, which was found to be perfectly shaped for the bath and which had tremendous vibrations. Through Her Divine Knowledge She has identified all the swayambhus, which are the edifices of vibration born by Mother Earth. She narrates the complete account of all the places blessed by the Goddess in all Her incarnations. For instance, in Maharashtra there are the three and half coils of the Kundalini and the eight swayambhus of Shri Ganesha. These are also called 'Peethas'.

She instantly recognises the statue of any deity and explains its special features which cannot be found in any book. Her divine knowledge is described as Nirmala Vidya. When She saw the temple of Athena in Athens, She recognised it as the Adi Shakti revealing that 'Atha' in sanskrit means Primordial, the goddess Athena carries the Kundalini in Her hand. The Yogis could feel tremendous vibrations from the temple. In the temple of Delphi She discovered the Swayambhu of Shri Ganesha which no one had ever noticed before. Greece was the Devaloka, but after the death of Socrates, people brought down the level of Gods from Dharma to Adharma. This was the real Greek tragedy.

Her divine form is seen in all the dimensions and sometimes by Her Grace, some Yogis have been able to see Her Divine aspect, Her face in the cloud or over a rainbow. Many miracle photographs have revealed Her various divine aspects.

Once after a Puja in Dharamsala, She revealed the vibrations emanating from the Himalayas and She also revealed that the Himalayas are a Swayambhu. Now vibrations are clearly visible in thousands of Her photographs. The camera is able to catch this subtle aspect better than the human eye. Some of these photographs show various Deities on Her chakras.

Nature responds particularly to vibrations. During a puja in the Alps there was such a raging storm and rain, the villagers feared that there would be a flood. A music programme was scheduled for the evening and there was no hope of any respite. Shri Mataji gave vibrations to the storm and within half an hour the sky cleared. She explains that vibrations have an in-built intelligence that connects with the all pervading consciousness, hence when you get connected to it, then everything in nature works for you.

During Her visit to Istanbul in November, 1994, the town was facing acute water shortage as there had been no rain and the Turkish Yogis prayed to Her. She gave vibrations to the problem and next morning it started raining so heavily and continued unabated for days. Nature gets very excited whenever She arrives in a new place. If it is warm then the temperature suddenly drops and vice versa.

There is usually a drizzle that welcome Her. She was addressing a seminar some thirty meters from the sea near Bombay. Suddenly the sea rose some thirty meters towards where She stood and touched Her feet, then receded. Thousands of yogis standing there witnessed the miracle in sheer amazement.

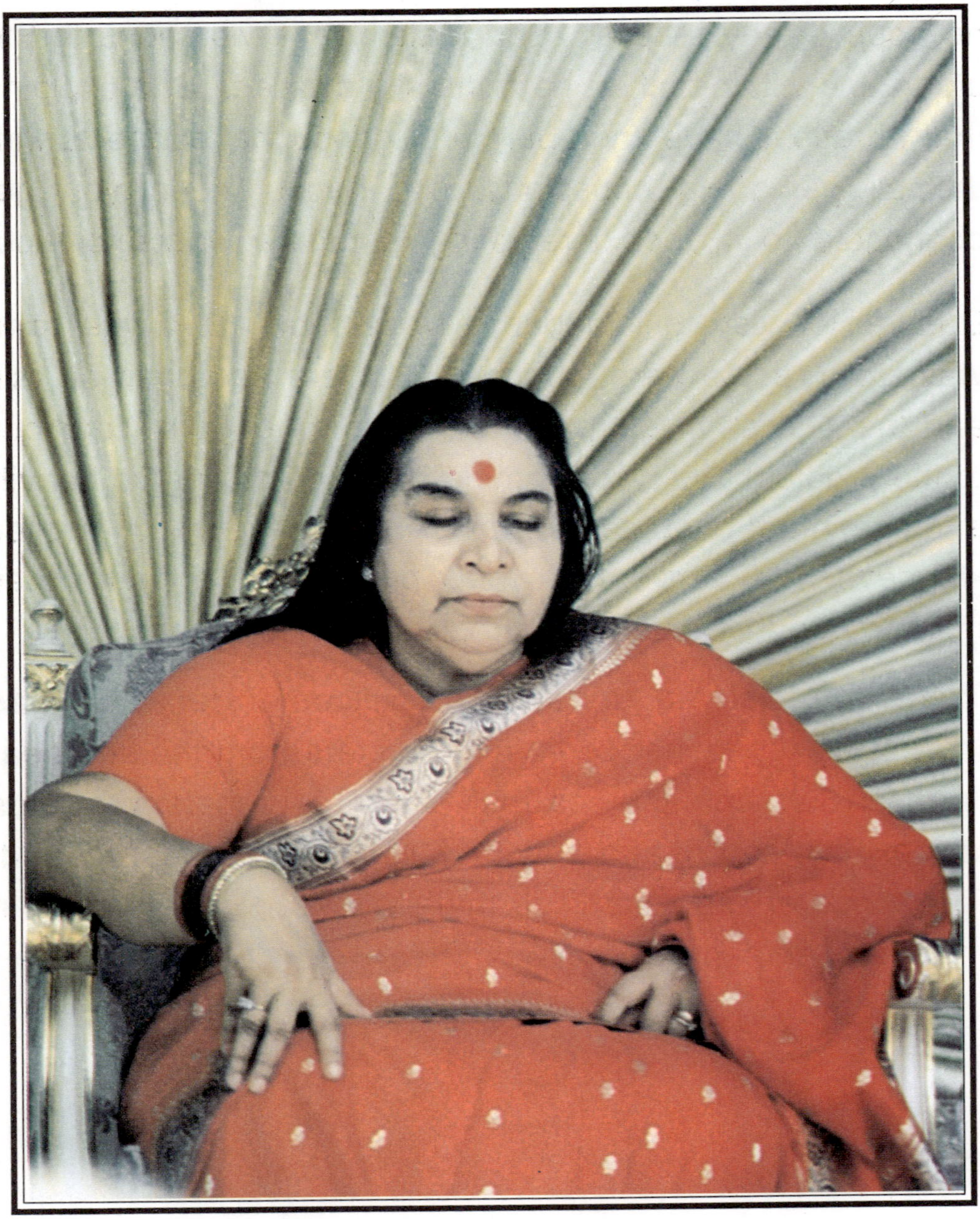

17

EPILOGUE

Shri Mataji is now seventy five years old, but recently a press reporter who saw Her in Turkey was so endeared by Her glowing face, that he reported in the morning newspaper that a young Messiah had come to save Turkey. Her global travel, for the spreading of Sahaja Yoga takes Her further than ever before. Between Her long travels She keeps very late hours to complete Her book called 'Meta Modernism.' Her soul stirring book 'Meta Modern Era' was released in October 1995. She initially wanted to express Her ocean of love and compassion, but felt that in the interest of the seekers it was first necessary to expose the myths and false identifications that have misled the seekers of modern times, so that they may see the reality. The other book would follow later.

Shri Mataji enjoys Her various enterprises to sponsor

ethnic handicrafts through Her import - export business. She creates porcelain designs and Her infinite talents can be seen in terracotta, wood and brass carvings from India, ceramics from Turkey, Porcelain from Russia and other countries - She teaches artisans how to overcome their conditionings and to become more versatile.

After setting up a primary school in Rome, a high school in Dharamsala, She is preparing the module for a Sahaja World University. Her plans for a Sahaja Yoga clinical research centre and a hospital for the poor are on the anvil. Politicians, businessmen, economists, scientists and doctors from all over the world seek Her advice.* She rises before dawn and works until the early hours of the morning, hardly sleeping for two - three hours. During Her India Tour She spends some time on Her Pune farm, making improvements, giving fresh ideas and developing new projects.

She has set up various NGO organisations all over the country to rehabilitate street children, abandoned and destitute women. She is greatly concerned about, Muslim divorced women who have been thrown out by their husbands in preference to other women under the so-called pronouncement of "Talak, Talak, Talak". Either these women starve or in sheer desperation they take to prostitution. She is busy setting up shelter and rehabilitation homes for them. She is deeply concerned about injustice to women and is making great effort for their relief through legislation. She is also working very hard for intercommunity harmony. An Islamic study group inspired by the teachings hosted a World Islamic Conference in Lucknow in February 1998 to foster peace and unity among all communities. The State Government greatly appreciated Her effort and have extended their cooperation for promoting Her work.

Her approach to all practical problems is through love. In an International conference in St. Petersburg most of the speakers had got lost in mental jargons. The organises wanted to reprimand them but She explained that it is better to show them the futility of their mental jargons, thus exposing the misidentifications while spontaneously dressing the ego.

Her compassion is such that even a correction is finely carried without fracturing the ego. This can only be achieved by great technique apart from compassion. She indoubtedly has a complete mastery of all these skills. There is no aggression in Her nature and yet She achieves everything with the power of Her love. From Her life we can clearly see how the power of love works. Many people cheated Her but She forgives them spontaneously. She never punishes anyone, Her love simply works out the correction.

She studied human beings in great depth and says that this human realisation was necessary of Her work. She is absolutely down to earth, saying we must see what the utility of the instrument is. If it has no utility then what is its use. With this detachment one can clearly see the futility in such a mental argument.

Himself the most decorated person in the world, Her husband said to Her, "actually you should be the one receiving all these awards;" "What for" She answered, "this is My love that is working, I have not paid for it, its just My love which pays me. This love is a feeling of oneness with all of you, your families, your countries - everything. Its something I always feel, that you are all a part and parcel of My being."

Her husband says that he never imagined that She could achieve so much in just twenty years - single handed. Indeed Her life reaffirms that the one who made this beautiful creation must have very carefully thought out everything and will not allow Her creation to be destroyed by any negative forces.

All the Sahaja Yogis become cells in Her body. If any Sahaja Yogi is troubled or sick, She feels it in Her body and takes on the pain and through Her power She cures the pain. At such a point Her physical body undergoes a physical change.

Her feet swell up and it becomes difficult for Her to walk. Gradually with a little massage, the vibrations are released and the feet once again become normal. She explains, "Any chakra you catch collectively, I get the problem and I have to solve it. It is a compulsion that I have to solve it. I have taken you into Myself."

One cannot imagine how much pain She bears for others. She silently takes on the pain of others and not a muscle on Her complain or talk of Her problems. She is so full of concern for others that every cell in Her body works for others. She never thinks about Herself. She feels that "loving others is much more fulfilling than loving oneself."

Perhaps this is as close as a mortal can even get towards witnessing divine miracles at work. In Her compassion She says that you should not feel bad that you are troubling Me. "It is My own, its My own doing, My own work and My own responsibility." From Her life one realises that life is not a battle between dharma and adharma, it is much more - it is love, joy; forgiveness. This cannot be learnt from any book or scripture, it is a living process; a feeling that grows from one soul to another. When the Kundalini rises this process of osmos takes place.

Indeed, from Her life one realises what "*Divine Love and Bliss*" really means, and one is spellbound by the wonderous beauty of **The Face of God.**

"I knew about myself since I was born. I have done nothing special. If I have done anything special it is to understand human beings, what's their problem. They followed Christ, they followed Mohammed Saheb, they followed Shri Krishna, but nothing penetrated inside. Why? - because they were not connected to the all pervading power. Then only what I have done is to work out the permutations and combinations of human beings. That's not difficult because there are mainly seven chakras that one has to work out and how you can raise the kundalini to break the sahasrara. It has worked and its working out in thousands."

18

APPENDIX

Letter to Mr. Gorbachev dated Aug 21, 1990

My humble plans for a future global system :

These are certain ideas I have for individual and social transformation after Sahaja Yoga has established awareness of 'collective consciousness'. (This is the state one achieves as a result of his internal transformation through Self-Realisation. He also feels the All-Pervading Power of Love that does all living work. As a result one sees the world as one nation, one sees one truth about human beings and their different ideologies. One develops a truly global perspective.

I believe that you are very much a person who can have

this perspective and that you can plan for our common future.

The state of 'collective consciousness' that I refer to will give us the sustaining strength and wisdom that we need in pursuit of global Government. Through this state of consciousness we can easily develop:

1) *A political system that will easily secure effective participation in decision-making, not according to selfish interest, but in accordance with the laws of truth.*

2) *A balanced economic system catering for the essential requirements of human consumption based on the barter system. A truly global system would provide the machinery for evaluating the right ratio of distribution according to supply and demand, but even more importantly, on a truly humanitarian basis.*

3) *A social system based on righteous and noble values can be developed without any problems or disharmony, because with collective consciousness each individual can feel contented only if the whole collective is contented.*

4) *The manufacture of machine-made goods should be balanced with hand-made products, with full consid-*

eration given to Mother Earth and ecological problems. If more artistic goods are produced, the consumption of matter will be less, because people will want to preserve such things.

5) *Technological systems can be worked out by truly benevolent scientists to provide for the essential, as well as the highest human needs, according to the law of benevolence, instead of enhancing so-called progress which is fuelled by the human weaknesses of lust and greed.*

6) *A global system can be set up to preserve all those cultures that are benevolent in nature and to foster mutual respect and co-operation between all kinds of races and cultures.*

7) *A global educational system can be made simpler for children and concentrate more on making them compassionate and dynamic proficient in their own language, as well as one or two international languages.*

8) *An administrative system can be developed that is run by mature, saintly people, who are flexible and have a capacity for self-correction.*

These idealistic ideas may sound fantastic and impracticable but with the dimensions that we touch in our awareness of collective consciousness, I have found from my personal experience that, they are in fact very easy to execute. In Sahaja Yoga we have thousands of Yogis from at least forty five nations and I have found out that these ideas are working very smoothly amongst them on a very down-to-earth level. Thus the ideals have become concrete truths in the light of glorious reality.

The door of Sahaja Yoga is open to everyone and every human being can achieve collective consciousness. The only problem is, that the freedom of choice of the individual has to be respected because he has ultimately to enter the area of total freedom. Thus there may be many who may not sincerely seek their salvation. But if later on they see the multitude of Realised Souls enjoying the bliss or collective consciousness, they may also desire to get in to their higher evolutionary process. This is how all evolutionary processes have worked in nature.

The guiding and controlling force that acts is the spirit. This is the collective being within us which manifests in our attention and makes us collectively conscious. We can then feel our subtle centres and those of others - <u>on our finger tips</u>. Once we learn how to correct them, we can easily overcome all our physical, mental, emotional and spiritual *problems. In this way we are creating a new angelic society which ultimately solves all man-made collective problems: Immorality and poverty, violence and corruption, destructive personal habits of human beings like alcoholism and drug abuse, problems of ecology, of economic exploitation and aggression, narrow nationalism, religious fundamentalism and the scourge of war. These are the cancers of modern times, because so-called human freedom has allowed man to blindly jump into a greater darkness of ignorance.*

<u>My humble suggestions for immediate measures</u> :

Privatisation of the production of consumer goods in bigger factories by making the workers shareholders. In smaller factories give full freedom to the workers to open new factories.

For very big industries that are not producing consumer goods, foreign collaboration should be secured with regard to technology, management and capital investment.

There should be an announcement of global policy, with the government concentrating on improving the infrastructure: transport, communications, energy, water, special courts for industrial arbitration and conciliation.

THE CONSTITUTION OF INDIA - PRESS RELEASE

On the occasion of Republic Day Shri Mataji Nirmala Devi was interviewed by foreign correspondents on the current controversy of Dr. Ambedkar and his role in the framing of the Indian Constitution.

Shri Mataji said, "No one person made the constitution. My father, the late Mr. P.K. Salve was also a member of the Constituent Assembly. He was a master of fourteen languages and translated the Koran into Hindi. He was the only member from minority community who was elected by general public and who was not on the minority ticket. Stalwarts like Krishnaswamy Aiyer was one of the most effective personalities. The drafting of the Constitution was not done by any single individual. Like My father, Dr. Ambedkar, was also on the minority committee. They were all of different ideologies.

Of course they had a right to draft the Constitution as members of the Constituent Assembly. But none of them had a right to pass remarks about Shri Rama and Shri Krishna. Unless and until one is a Saint and has that deep spiritual insight, it is impossible for one to envisage the manifestation of a divine incarnation and His life.

As Saints cannot change the Constitution, the members of the Constituent Assembly have no right to change what the Saints have said about Shri Rama and Shri Krishna. Such an endeavour by them could be judged as an unauthorised aggression. But in this world there is no restrictions for people who want to take the divine laws into their hands. Still no one has the right to hurt the feelings of millions of people all over the world.

Saints have vehemently refuted and have laboured ardently to remove the evil and misleading customs of the masses, but they never arrogantly found faults with incarnations as the intellectuals do with their egos. I agree that by making too much ado about this trifling thought, people have given it unnecessary importance and publicity. It was very unwise, indiscrete and dangerous. Nobody was aware of these damaging remarks in the riddles, and of course it makes no difference at all to the incarnations and their pure divinity.

It was very indiscrete to publicise it to such an extent, because it will only give justification to people who indulge into the growing vices of drinking and womanising. Moreover, the new generation will have no ideals to look forward to anymore, and they may get lost as the hippies or the drug addicts of the West do. These are very crucial times when we need sensible people to guide our children, as the value system is getting very corrupt.

It is a joke, the way in our country people unite on both sides to fight each other, on issues which are frivolous and nonsensical. I wish they could unite for good and constructive work, of removing ills of our society and rebuilding it on moral values, to pay their homages and respects to their loving Creator.

KNIGHTHOOD FOR MR. C.P. SRIVASTAVA

By L.K. SHARMA,
The Times of India News Service

LONDON, July 9, 1990.

Mr. C.P. Srivastava, former secretary-general of the International Maritime Organisation, received recognition from Britain for his contribution to world shipping when the Queen conferred on him honorary knighthood.

Mr. Srivastava is perhaps the first Indian since the country's independence to have been awarded the title of "Knight commander of the most distinguished order of St. Michael and St. George". He received the insignia at a dinner hosted today by the government, at which the transport secretary, Mr. Cecil Parkinson, lauded his role as the secretary-general of the IMO. Other recipients of an honorary knighthood in the recent past include Mr. Ronald Reagan and the violinist Yehudi Menuhin.

Mr. Srivastava was first elected to the IMO, a U.N. agency based in London, in 1974, and served four successive terms till December last year. The assembly of IMO lauded his pioneering role in the *establishment of the World Maritime University in Sweden with branches in several countries, an international maritime academy in Italy and an International Maritime Law Institute in Malta.*

Mr. Srivastava's diplomatic feat was not to let the organisation be dragged into any controversy. He told this reporter that his most satisfying experience was to have been trusted equally by both developed and developing countries. Shipping being a high-technology industry, developing countries had to strive hard to increase their share in world shipping. This share had gone up over the years from six per cent to about 25 per cent, he said.

Mr. Srivastava's long years as the secretary-general of the IMO saw its expansion and universal acceptance for its conventions and protocols promoting the objectives of the organisation for safer shipping and cleaner oceans. He was responsible for implementing a programme of technical co-operation intended to make developing countries more self-reliant in the maritime sector. Mr. Srivastava is currently chancellor of the Maritime University.

Awards and honours are not new for Mr. Srivastava and his room is full of sashes and insignia, having received the highest civilian awards from the governments of countries, including West Germany, Egypt, Sweden, Norway, France and Poland. He started his career as a civil servant and as under-secretary in the ministry of commerce.

After brief stints in the district administration in Meerut and Lucknow and in the directorate-general of shipping, Mr. Srivastava became the first chief executive of the Shipping Corporation of India (SCI) and guided it through its formative years. Mr. Srivastava was awarded Padma Bhushan in 1972 for his contributions in establishing one of the most successful public sector undertakings.

In-between two stints at the SCL, he served Mr. Lal Bahadur Shastri as joint secretary in the newly-formed prime minister's secretariat. He was in Moscow when Mr. Shastri died.

Dr Mehdi Rouhani

Chief Spiritual de la
Commu Musubrane Chaite in Europe
Secretariat:
16, Av. du PRESIDENT KENNEDY
PARIS 75016

To Her Excellency, Her Holiness Shri Mataji Nirmala Devi, President of the universal and spiritual movement of Sahaja Yoga.

It is with truly profound respect and heartfelt joy that I offer to You, all my sincere felicitations for this grand birthday of Yours, this tremendous day of Your birth which exactly corresponds with the New Year which our ancient nation of Iran is about to celebrate, according to her ancestral traditions.

You have dedicated your entire life to the establishment of morality and to the evolution of the consciousness of humanity through love and compassion with the aim of self knowledge.

You have for this, founded a movement which all we Muslims believe to be a teaching whose ultimate goal is the knowledge of God.

Has not the Prophet proclaimed:

"He who knows himself, knows God"?

It is obvious that humanity will not find fulfilment until they have established the balance between the material world and spirituality.

If one glances through the combined history and culture of our two countries, Iran and India, we can easily perceive that these two nations have offered humanity similar civilisations and have continually raised the flag of peace and peaceful combination throughout the world. We still need today to continue their historia miscian.

I am convinced that by constant effort and commitment, we can, You and I, transform this sacred and ancient dream into reality.

Thus we must permit all those who are trapped within the wheels and machinery of Western civilisation, to lighten the loads on their lives; to establish themselves in morality and to warm their hearts with the joy of spiritual life.

In closing I would like to express to You my intense feelings of gratitute and recognition, which I know are shared by all the Muslims of Europe, and in particular the Shiite community, for all Your effort and sacrifice in the pursuit of peace.

It is my humble wish that this gratitude and recognition which I hold for You, be conveyed to the government and the people of India.

.Ayatollah Dr Mehdi Rouhani

She never thinks of herself as some one special or superior. - She instantly strikes a conversation with a fellow traveller, a farmer, a driver, anybody. She is not conscious of anybody's status, importance or money. She is such a genuinely simple and a kind person; on Her seventy second birthday She remarked, "I don't know what to say on my birthday which comes and goes and comes and goes. Seventy two years have passed, I don't think about it. I also don't feel my age at all in any way, because I don't think about it. It is there, till I have to live, I live. When I don't have to live I won't live, that's all! - it's not my job. If there is anything my love wants to do is to give realisation to everyone in the world, wherever they are."